TORAH PORTIONS WORKBOOK
EXODUS

THIS WORKBOOK BELONGS TO:

_____

Proverbs 22:6 "Train up a child in the way he should go: and when he is old, he will not depart from it."

©2017 TORAH TOWN
Gary A. Arbaugh
Fay A. Arbaugh

Deuteronomy 6:5-9 "Love the Lord your God with all your heart, with all your soul, and with all your strength. Take to heart these words that I give you today. Repeat them to your children. Talk about them when you're at home or away, when you lie down or get up. Write them down, and tie them around your wrist, and wear them as headbands as a reminder. Write them on the door frames of your houses and on your gates."

Deuteronomy 4:9-10 "But watch out! Be careful never to forget what you yourself have seen. Do not let these memories escape from your mind as long as you live! And be sure to pass them on to your children and grandchildren. Never forget the day when you stood before the Lord your God at Mount Sinai, where he told me, Summon the people before me, and I will personally instruct them. Then they will learn to fear me as long as they live, and they will teach their children to fear me also."

Deuteronomy 11:19 Teach them to your children. "Talk about them when you are at home and when you are on the road, when you are going to bed and when you are getting up."

Matthew 19:13-15 "One day some parents brought their children to Yeshua so he could lay his hands on them and pray for them. But the disciples scolded the parents for bothering him. But Yeshua said, "Let the children come to me. Don't stop them! For the Kingdom of Heaven belongs to those who are like these children." And he placed his hands on their heads and blessed them before he left."

Proverbs 20:11 "Even a child makes himself known by his doings, whether his work is pure, and whether it is right."

We can all agree that we see things around us changing rapidly as the "end times" are nearing. We see that in order for our children to be spiritually grounded in their faith and able to fight the spiritual battles that lay ahead they need to be prepared.

We would all like to be able to shelter our children from what lies ahead and protect them from all the "bad" around them. But really, if we equip them with God's Word, and teach them the love of Yeshua, what better gift could we give them.

We feel strongly that to **"train up a child in the way he should go..."** they need to be present. They need to hear what the Scriptures say, and feel as if they are a part of the reason that they are going to study. They should also feel comfortable enough that if they desire to participate in a group discussion that they are able. We do understand that getting children involved has it's challenges, and this is not something that happens at one meeting. It takes time and patience on EVERYONES part. Even those who do not have children can help. We are a body of believers and all aspects of that body should be working together as a whole.

FELLOWSHIP LEADERS:

What can you do for your group to help the children want to be more involved?

- Do you give children an opportunity to read (shorter broken down segments) during meeting.
- Do you ask them for assistance in setting up chairs or distributing handouts?
- Can you come up with some more simplistic questions for children to answer during that weeks Torah portion? What was Abraham's sons name? How many of each animal was on the Arc? Etc.
- Is there a child that would like to say a prayer?

THOSE ATTENDING WITHOUT CHILDREN:

- Do you have a listening ear?
- Do you have songs to sing or stories to tell that children would like to hear?
- Could you "adopt" a child for a day? Sit with them, help them to pay attention or to listen?

OTHER SUGGESTIONS:

- **Adults:** Make "deeper" topic notes during the study/bible reading while children are present...once you are finished, excuse the children if they want to then go play or have desert. Everyone takes a short break, then if there are "deeper" things that others would like to discuss you can do that while children are playing. Not everything is child appropriate, so this will offer adults an opportunity to discuss further the scriptures or topics they desire.

- After study, commend the children that participated...tell them what a good job they did with their reading, or how much you liked their comments or prayer.

- **Children/Teens:** Encourage your child to associate with "older" ones attending.

- Encourage your child to get to know those in the group better...ask them questions about when they were kids, how were things different. What are some of their hobbies or interest?

- Is there something your child can do to help those who are elderly? Get them a drink...carry their bags to the car for them. etc.

We realize that there are many different situations and circumstances that parents and grandparents and fellowships deal with regarding this issue and nothing is black and white. Children learn in many different ways, and a 14 year old is not going to have the same interest as a 4 year old, but there are countless ways that we can incorporate our children of all ages to be present during the Bible Study. Some of these may be things you already do, but it may also be a way that we can all work together to help each other in love.

Even if your study currently does things a certain way, maybe you can offer some suggestions to the group or come up with your own ideas or ways to incorporate children into your home study. This may be a little more different than what you have done in the past or are currently doing, but if everyone has the same goal in mind, which is to bring up our children to a deeper understanding and greater knowledge of God's word, then it will be worth it, we will have WON the battle!

Torah Town has put together this booklet as a tool to help Parents, Fellowship Leaders, and even those of the home study family that don't have children. We have tried to incorporate something for all ages and interest. We pray that this will be a blessing to everyone young and old.

And, as always, feel free to make as many copies as you need and share them with others.

To the Parents:

This workbook is designed to enhance your child's learning and participation during Your Community Fellowship Meetings and throughout the week leading up to each Sabbath. In it you will find many activities for each parsha segment, including verses from the Prophets and the New Testament that we pray will both stimulate the mind and keep little hands busy.

You will find each Torah Portion is broken down into daily readings. You may decide on using the Torah Portions in this book as a homeschooling tool. The World English Bible (WEB) is used throughout and we have changed Yahweh to YHWH to allow for your personal interpretation of the Name. We chose this version since it is easily read and can be understood by younger children.

Each Torah Portion has one or more **highlighted text** pertaining to a concept, idea or commandment, and are for spurring thought, verbal interaction and participation.

About Our Activities and Games:

MAKE A MARK – Is a listening game to see how many times someone in the assembly says certain words. This will instill good listening habits along with paying attention to the Torah Reading.

FIRST FIND – This is a Scripture Hunting game that will build knowledge of the location of Bible Books and increase participation in the Bible Study. Allow them to read the passage they find and have a special treat or small gift like scripture pencils to give to whoever finds the passage first.

COLORING PAGE – Each Coloring page is based on the weekly Torah Portion. Allow them to color while listening to the Bible Study. Children are great multi-taskers and you will be surprised at how much they absorb.

WORD FIND – Is the standard word search game where each word is based on the Parsha reading. Aimed at the older children to keep them interested in the topics presented each week.

CROSSWORD – For more advanced or older children. As with all other activities, it is based on the weekly Torah Portion, Prophets or New Testament verses for that week.

VERSE FIND – The letters are scrambled below a grid. The object is to solve in order to know the contents of the verse. (The Answer is Provided in the Title)

SCRAMBLE – Several words are scrambled and in order to solve the puzzle. Once the words are discovered, match the corresponding number with the letter to find the hidden phrase.

HIDDEN VERSE – Solve the hidden verse by finding the words in the list and then copy the remaining letters in order on the lines provided. (The Answer is Provided in the Title)

"Children are great imitators. So give them something great to imitate."

TABLE OF CONTENTS
World English Bible* used throughout
Yahweh changed to YHWH to allow for your personal interpretation of the Name

SHEMOT (EXODUS)

WEEK	PARSHA NAME	ENGLISH	PORTION	PAGE
13	Shemot שְׁמוֹת	Names	Ex. 1:1 - 6:1	6
14	Va'eira וָאֵרָא	Appeared	Ex. 6:2 - 9:35	19
15	Bo בֹּא	Come!	Ex. 10:1 - 13:16	31
16	Beshaiach בְּשַׁלַּח	When he sent out	Ex. 13:17 - 17:16	44
17	Yitro יִתְרוֹ	Jethro	Ex. 18:1 - 20:26	56
18	Mishpatim מִשְׁפָּטִים	Laws	Ex. 21:1 - 24:18	65
19	Terumah תְּרוּמָה	Offering	Ex. 25:1 - 27:19	77
20	Tetzaveh תְּצַוֶּה	You shall command	Ex. 27:20 - 30:10	88
21	Ki Tisa כִּי תִשָּׂא	When you elevate	Ex. 30:11 - 34:35	99
22	Vayakhel וַיַּקְהֵל	And he assembled	Ex. 35:1 - 38:20	113
23	Pekudei פְקוּדֵי	Accountings	Ex. 38:21 - 40:38	125

SHEMOT
שְׁמוֹת
EXODUS

It Means: **NAMES**

Our Thirteenth Torah Portion is called Shemot! שְׁמוֹת
Exodus 1:1 – Exodus 6:1
PROPHETS: Isaiah 27:6-28:13; 29:22-23
NEW TESTAMENT: Matthew 22:23-46; Luke 5:12-39;
Acts 3:12-15, 5:27-32, 7:17-36, 22:1-22, 24:11-16; Hebrews 11:23-26

MAKE A MARK

Each time you hear someone say one of the words below make a '/" beside the word. See how many marks you can get!

tribes	
Moses	
made	
Pharaoh	
slaves	
work	

FIRST FIND

~

If someone mentions a verse or scripture that is NOT in this Torah Portion, see if YOU can be the First to Find it!

SHEMOT - Names

```
R V M D B S Z F O S F H D S A
S E G O E L L W E E I O H K A
N P T S T O O T F H R A E C R
C I O S C H I O D S S R B I O
O M A K A L E X D U T A R R N
D R S T E M L R H R B H E B G
G A H A N S K K U L O P W N H
W A R T S U M S Z U R H I O W
V S P J E B O A A B N N S P H
I X A X D J U M N T R D S U Y
S A C R I F I C E U H O R E B
S E R P E N T O B N A I D I M
J D P V J S S E N R E D L I W
F Q B Q Q X W V P S Q Y D Q L
N A I T P Y G E E R H U F M U
```

MOSES	HOREB	SERPENT
MOTHER	BURNING	BLOOD
EGYPTIAN	BUSH	AARON
HEBREW	YHWH	SPOKESMAN
PHARAOH	BULRUSHES	FIRSTBORN
FLOCKS	ISRAELITE	STRAW
MIDIAN	WILDERNESS	BRICKS
JETHRO	SACRIFICE	TASKMASTER
MOUNTAIN	ROD	

Israel Increases Greatly in Egypt

SUNDAY Exo 1:1 Now these are the names of the sons of Israel, who came into Egypt (every man and his household came with Jacob):

Exo 1:2 Reuben, Simeon, Levi, and Judah,

Exo 1:3 Issachar, Zebulun, and Benjamin,

Exo 1:4 Dan and Naphtali, Gad and Asher.

Exo 1:5 All the souls who came out of Jacob's body were seventy souls, and Joseph was in Egypt already.

Exo 1:6 Joseph died, as did all his brothers, and all that generation.

Exo 1:7 **The children of Israel were fruitful, and increased abundantly, and multiplied, and grew exceedingly mighty; and the land was filled with them.**

Pharaoh Oppresses Israel

Exo 1:8 Now there arose a new king over Egypt, who didn't know Joseph.

Exo 1:9 He said to his people, "Behold, the people of the children of Israel are more and mightier than we.

Exo 1:10 Come, let's deal wisely with them, lest they multiply, and it happen that when any war breaks out, they also join themselves to our enemies, and fight against us, and escape out of the land."

Exo 1:11 Therefore they set taskmasters over them to afflict them with their burdens. They built storage cities for Pharaoh: Pithom and Raamses.

Exo 1:12 But the more they afflicted them, the more they multiplied and the more they spread out. They were grieved because of the children of Israel.

Exo 1:13 The Egyptians ruthlessly made the children of Israel serve,

Exo 1:14 and they made their lives bitter with hard service, in mortar and in brick, and in all kinds of service in the field, all their service, in which they ruthlessly made them serve.

Exo 1:15 The king of Egypt spoke to the Hebrew midwives, of whom the name of the one was Shiphrah, and the name of the other Puah,

Exo 1:16 and he said, "When you perform the duty of a midwife to the Hebrew women, and see them on the birth stool; if it is a son, then you shall kill him; but if it is a daughter, then she shall live."

Exo 1:17 But the midwives feared God, and didn't do what the king of Egypt commanded them, but saved the baby boys alive.

MONDAY Exo 1:18 The king of Egypt called for the midwives, and said to them, "Why have you done this thing, and have saved the boys alive?"

Exo 1:19 The midwives said to Pharaoh, "Because the Hebrew women aren't like the Egyptian women; for they are vigorous, and give birth before the midwife comes to them."

Exo 1:20 **God dealt well with the midwives, and the people multiplied, and grew very mighty.**

Exo 1:21 Because the midwives feared God, he gave them families.

Exo 1:22 Pharaoh commanded all his people, saying, "You shall cast every son who is born into the river, and every daughter you shall save alive."

The Birth of Moses

Exo 2:1 A man of the house of Levi went and took a daughter of Levi as his wife.

Exo 2:2 The woman conceived, and bore a son. When she saw that he was a fine child, she hid him three months.

Exo 2:3 When she could no longer hide him, she took a papyrus basket for him, and coated it with tar and with pitch. She put the child in it, and laid it in the reeds by the river's bank.

Exo 2:4 His sister stood far off, to see what would be done to him.

Exo 2:5 Pharaoh's daughter came down to bathe at the river. Her maidens walked along by the riverside. She saw the basket among the reeds, and sent her servant to get it.

Exo 2:6 She opened it, and saw the child, and behold, the baby cried. She had compassion on him, and said, "This is one of the Hebrews' children."

Exo 2:7 Then his sister said to Pharaoh's daughter, "Should I go and call a nurse for you from the Hebrew women, that she may nurse the child for you?"

Exo 2:8 Pharaoh's daughter said to her, "Go." The young woman went and called the child's mother.

Exo 2:9 Pharaoh's daughter said to her, "Take this child away, and nurse him for me, and I will give you your wages." The woman took the child, and nursed it.

Exo 2:10 **The child grew, and she brought him to Pharaoh's daughter, and he became her son. She named him Moses, and said, "Because I drew him out of the water."**

Moses Flees to Midian

TUESDAY Exo 2:11 In those days, when Moses had grown up, he went out to his brothers, and looked at their burdens. He saw an Egyptian striking a Hebrew, one of his brothers.

Exo 2:12 He looked this way and that way, and when he saw that there was no one, he killed the Egyptian, and hid him in the sand.

Exo 2:13 He went out the second day, and behold, two men of the Hebrews were fighting with each other. He said to him who did the wrong, "Why do you strike your fellow?"

Exo 2:14 He said, "Who made you a prince and a judge over us? Do you plan to kill me, as you killed the Egyptian?" Moses was afraid, and said, "Surely this thing is known."

Exo 2:15 **Now when Pharaoh heard this thing, he sought to kill Moses. But Moses fled from the face of Pharaoh, and lived in the land of Midian, and he sat down by a well.**

Exo 2:16 Now the priest of Midian had seven daughters. They came and drew water, and filled the troughs to water their father's flock.

Exo 2:17 The shepherds came and drove them away; but Moses stood up and helped them, and watered their flock.

Exo 2:18 When they came to Reuel, their father, he said, "How is it that you have returned so early today?"

Exo 2:19 They said, "An Egyptian delivered us out of the hand of the shepherds, and moreover he drew water for us, and watered the flock."

Exo 2:20 He said to his daughters, "Where is he? Why is it that you have left the man? Call him, that he may eat bread."

Exo 2:21 Moses was content to dwell with the man. He gave Moses Zipporah, his daughter.

Exo 2:22 She bore a son, and he named him Gershom, for he said, "I have lived as a foreigner in a foreign land."

God Hears Israel's Groaning

Exo 2:23 In the course of those many days, the king of Egypt died, and the children of Israel sighed because of the bondage, and they cried, and their cry came up to God because of the bondage.

Exo 2:24 God heard their groaning, and God remembered his covenant with Abraham, with Isaac, and with Jacob.

Exo 2:25 God saw the children of Israel, and God was concerned about them.

The Burning Bush

WEDNESDAY Exo 3:1 Now Moses was keeping the flock of Jethro, his father-in-law, the priest of Midian, and he led the flock to the back of the wilderness, and came to God's mountain, to Horeb.

Exo 3:2 YHWH's angel appeared to him in a flame of fire out of the middle of a bush. He looked, and behold, the bush burned with fire, and the bush was not consumed.

Exo 3:3 Moses said, "I will go now, and see this great sight, why the bush is not burned."

Exo 3:4 When YHWH saw that he came over to see, God called to him out of the middle of the bush, and said, "Moses! Moses!" He said, "Here I am."

Exo 3:5 He said, "Don't come close. Take off your sandals, for the place you are standing on is holy ground."

Exo 3:6 ***Moreover he said, "I am the God of your father, the God of Abraham, the God of Isaac, and the God of Jacob." Moses hid his face; for he was afraid to look at God.***

Exo 3:7 YHWH said, "I have surely seen the affliction of my people who are in Egypt, and have heard their cry because of their taskmasters, for I know their sorrows.

Exo 3:8 I have come down to deliver them out of the hand of the Egyptians, and to bring them up out of that land to a good and large land, to a land flowing with milk and honey; to the place of the Canaanite, the Hittite, the Amorite, the Perizzite, the Hivite, and the Jebusite.

Exo 3:9 Now, behold, the cry of the children of Israel has come to me. Moreover I have seen the oppression with which the Egyptians oppress them.

Exo 3:10 Come now therefore, and I will send you to Pharaoh, that you may bring my people, the children of Israel, out of Egypt."

Exo 3:11 Moses said to God, "Who am I, that I should go to Pharaoh, and that I should bring the children of Israel out of Egypt?"

Exo 3:12 He said, "Certainly I will be with you. This will be the token to you, that I have sent you: when you have brought the people out of Egypt, you shall serve God on this mountain."

Exo 3:13 Moses said to God, "Behold, when I come to the children of Israel, and tell them, 'The God of your fathers has sent me to you;' and they ask me, 'What is his name?' What should I tell them?"

Exo 3:14 God said to Moses, "I AM WHO I AM," and he said, "You shall tell the children of Israel this: 'I AM has sent me to you.'"

Exo 3:15 God said moreover to Moses, "You shall tell the children of Israel this, 'YHWH, the God of your fathers, the God of Abraham, the God of Isaac, and the God of Jacob, has sent me to you.' This is my name forever, and this is my memorial to all generations.

THURSDAY Exo 3:16 Go and gather the elders of Israel together, and tell them, 'YHWH, the God of your fathers, the God of Abraham, of Isaac, and of Jacob, has appeared to me, saying, "I have surely visited you, and seen that which is done to you in Egypt;

MY NOTES

Exo 3:17 and I have said, I will bring you up out of the affliction of Egypt to the land of the Canaanite, the Hittite, the Amorite, the Perizzite, the Hivite, and the Jebusite, to a land flowing with milk and honey.'"

Exo 3:18 They will listen to your voice, and you shall come, you and the elders of Israel, to the king of Egypt, and you shall tell him, 'YHWH, the God of the Hebrews, has met with us. Now please let us go three days' journey into the wilderness, that we may sacrifice to YHWH, our God.'

Exo 3:19 I know that the king of Egypt won't give you permission to go, no, not by a mighty hand.

Exo 3:20 I will reach out my hand and strike Egypt with all my wonders which I will do among them, and after that he will let you go.

Exo 3:21 ***I will give this people favor in the sight of the Egyptians, and it will happen that when you go, you shall not go empty-handed.***

Exo 3:22 But every woman shall ask of her neighbor, and of her who visits her house, jewels of silver, jewels of gold, and clothing; and you shall put them on your sons, and on your daughters. You shall plunder the Egyptians."

Moses Given Powerful Signs

Exo 4:1 Moses answered, "But, behold, they will not believe me, nor listen to my voice; for they will say, 'YHWH has not appeared to you.'"

Exo 4:2 YHWH said to him, "What is that in your hand?" He said, "A rod."

Exo 4:3 He said, "Throw it on the ground." He threw it on the ground, and it became a snake; and Moses ran away from it.

Exo 4:4 YHWH said to Moses, "Stretch out your hand, and take it by the tail." He stretched out his hand, and took hold of it, and it became a rod in his hand.

Exo 4:5 "That they may believe that YHWH, the God of their fathers, the God of Abraham, the God of Isaac, and the God of Jacob, has appeared to you."

Exo 4:6 YHWH said furthermore to him, "Now put your hand inside your cloak." He put his hand inside his cloak, and when he took it out, behold, his hand was leprous, as white as snow.

Exo 4:7 He said, "Put your hand inside your cloak again." He put his hand inside his cloak again, and when he took it out of his cloak, behold, it had turned again as his other flesh.

Exo 4:8 "It will happen, if they will not believe you or listen to the voice of the first sign, that they will believe the voice of the latter sign.

Exo 4:9 It will happen, if they will not believe even these two signs or listen to your voice, that you shall take of the water of the river, and pour it on the dry land. The water which you take out of the river will become blood on the dry land."

Exo 4:10 Moses said to YHWH, "O Lord, I am not eloquent, neither before now, nor since you have spoken to your servant; for I am slow of speech, and of a slow tongue."

Exo 4:11 YHWH said to him, "Who made man's mouth? Or who makes one mute, or deaf, or seeing, or blind? Isn't it I, YHWH?

Exo 4:12 Now therefore go, and I will be with your mouth, and teach you what you shall speak."

Exo 4:13 He said, "Oh, Lord, please send someone else."

Exo 4:14 YHWH's anger burned against Moses, and he said, "What about Aaron, your brother, the Levite? I know that he can speak well. Also, behold, he comes out to meet you. When he sees you, he will be glad in his heart.

Exo 4:15 You shall speak to him, and put the words in his mouth. I will be with your mouth, and with his mouth, and will teach you what you shall do.

Exo 4:16 He will be your spokesman to the people; and it will happen, that he will be to you a mouth, and you will be to him as God.

Exo 4:17 You shall take this rod in your hand, with which you shall do the signs."

Moses Returns to Egypt

FRIDAY Exo 4:18 Moses went and returned to Jethro his father-in-law, and said to him, "Please let me go and return to my brothers who are in Egypt, and see whether they are still alive." Jethro said to Moses, "Go in peace."

Exo 4:19 YHWH said to Moses in Midian, "Go, return into Egypt; for all the men who sought your life are dead."

Exo 4:20 **Moses took his wife and his sons, and set them on a donkey, and he returned to the land of Egypt. Moses took God's rod in his hand.**

Exo 4:21 YHWH said to Moses, "When you go back into Egypt, see that you do before Pharaoh all the wonders which I have put in your hand, but I will harden his heart and he will not let the people go.

Exo 4:22 You shall tell Pharaoh, 'YHWH says, Israel is my son, my firstborn,

Exo 4:23 and I have said to you, "Let my son go, that he may serve me;" and you have refused to let him go. Behold, I will kill your son, your firstborn.'"

Exo 4:24 On the way at a lodging place, YHWH met Moses and wanted to kill him.

Exo 4:25 Then Zipporah took a flint, and cut off the foreskin of her son, and cast it at his feet; and she said, "Surely you are a bridegroom of blood to me."

Exo 4:26 So he let him alone. Then she said, "You are a bridegroom of blood," because of the circumcision.

Exo 4:27 YHWH said to Aaron, "Go into the wilderness to meet Moses." He went, and met him on God's mountain, and kissed him.

Exo 4:28 Moses told Aaron all YHWH's words with which he had sent him, and all the signs with which he had instructed him.

Exo 4:29 Moses and Aaron went and gathered together all the elders of the children of Israel.

Exo 4:30 Aaron spoke all the words which YHWH had spoken to Moses, and did the signs in the sight of the people.

Exo 4:31 The people believed, and when they heard that YHWH had visited the children of Israel, and that he had seen their affliction, then they bowed their heads and worshiped.

Making Bricks Without Straw

__SABBATH__ Exo 5:1 Afterward Moses and Aaron came, and said to Pharaoh, "This is what YHWH, the God of Israel, says, 'Let my people go, that they may hold a feast to me in the wilderness.'"

Exo 5:2 **Pharaoh said, "Who is YHWH, that I should listen to his voice to let Israel go? I don't know YHWH, and moreover I will not let Israel go."**

Exo 5:3 They said, "The God of the Hebrews has met with us. Please let us go three days' journey into the wilderness, and sacrifice to YHWH, our God, lest he fall on us with pestilence, or with the sword."

Exo 5:4 The king of Egypt said to them, "Why do you, Moses and Aaron, take the people from their work? Get back to your burdens!"

Exo 5:5 Pharaoh said, "Behold, the people of the land are now many, and you make them rest from their burdens."

Exo 5:6 The same day Pharaoh commanded the taskmasters of the people, and their officers, saying,

Exo 5:7 "You shall no longer give the people straw to make brick, as before. Let them go and gather straw for themselves.

Exo 5:8 The number of the bricks, which they made before, you require from them. You shall not diminish anything of it, for they are idle; therefore they cry, saying, 'Let's go and sacrifice to our God.'

Exo 5:9 Let heavier work be laid on the men, that they may labor in it; and don't let them pay any attention to lying words."

Exo 5:10 The taskmasters of the people went out, and their officers, and they spoke to the people, saying, "This is what Pharaoh says: 'I will not give you straw.

Exo 5:11 Go yourselves, get straw where you can find it, for nothing of your work shall be diminished.'"

Exo 5:12 So the people were scattered abroad throughout all the land of Egypt to gather stubble for straw.

Exo 5:13 The taskmasters were urgent saying, "Fulfill your work quota daily, as when there was straw!"

Exo 5:14 The officers of the children of Israel, whom Pharaoh's taskmasters had set over them, were beaten, and demanded, "Why haven't you fulfilled your quota both yesterday and today, in making brick as before?"

Exo 5:15 Then the officers of the children of Israel came and cried to Pharaoh, saying, "Why do you deal this way with your servants?

Exo 5:16 No straw is given to your servants, and they tell us, 'Make brick!' and behold, your servants are beaten; but the fault is in your own people."

Exo 5:17 But he said, "You are idle! You are idle! Therefore you say, 'Let's go and sacrifice to YHWH.'

Exo 5:18 Go therefore now, and work, for no straw shall be given to you, yet you shall deliver the same number of bricks!"

Exo 5:19 The officers of the children of Israel saw that they were in trouble, when it was said, "You shall not diminish anything from your daily quota of bricks!"

Exo 5:20 They met Moses and Aaron, who stood in the way, as they came out from Pharaoh:

Exo 5:21 and they said to them, "May YHWH look at you, and judge, because you have made us a stench to be abhorred in the eyes of Pharaoh, and in the eyes of his servants, to put a sword in their hand to kill us."

Exo 5:22 Moses returned to YHWH, and said, "Lord, why have you brought trouble on this people? Why is it that you have sent me?

Exo 5:23 For since I came to Pharaoh to speak in your name, he has brought trouble on this people; and you have not rescued your people at all."

God Promises Deliverance

Exo 6:1 **YHWH said to Moses, "Now you shall see what I will do to Pharaoh, for by a strong hand he shall let them go, and by a strong hand he shall drive them out of his land."**

CRYPTOGRAM – EXODUS 2:10

LETTER TILES – EXODUS 2:24

AB	AND	WI	NIN	G,	GO	COB	RAH
AN	HEI	RED	ROA	NAN	JA	T W	MBE
ISA	GO	HI	TH	D H	R G	D R	ITH
AM,	AND	S C	D T	D W	EME	AC,	EAR
ITH	OVE	.					

VA'EIRA

וָאֵרָא

EXODUS

It Means: APPEARED

Our Fourteenth Torah Portion is called Va'eira! וָאֵרָא
Exodus 6:2 – Exodus 9:35
PROPHETS: Ezekiel 28:25 - 29:21
NEW TESTAMENT: Romans 9:14-26; 2 Corinthians 6:14 - 7:1; Revelation 6:1-17, 8:1-13;16:1-21

MAKE A MARK

Each time you hear someone say one of the words below make a '/" beside the word. See how many marks you can get!

heart
plagues
blood
people
hard
Israelites

FIRST FIND

~

If someone mentions a verse or scripture that is NOT in this Torah Portion, see if YOU can be the First to Find it!

SUNDAY Exo 6:2 *God spoke to Moses, and said to him, "I am YHWH;*

Exo 6:3 and I appeared to Abraham, to Isaac, and to Jacob, as God Almighty; but by my name YHWH I was not known to them.

Exo 6:4 I have also established my covenant with them, to give them the land of Canaan, the land of their travels, in which they lived as aliens.

Exo 6:5 *Moreover I have heard the groaning of the children of Israel, whom the Egyptians keep in bondage, and I have remembered my covenant.*

Exo 6:6 Therefore tell the children of Israel, 'I am YHWH, and I will bring you out from under the burdens of the Egyptians, and I will rid you out of their bondage, and I will redeem you with an outstretched arm, and with great judgments:

Exo 6:7 and I will take you to me for a people, and I will be to you a God; and you shall know that I am YHWH your God, who brings you out from under the burdens of the Egyptians.

Exo 6:8 I will bring you into the land which I swore to give to Abraham, to Isaac, and to Jacob; and I will give it to you for a heritage: I am YHWH.'"

Exo 6:9 Moses spoke so to the children of Israel, but they didn't listen to Moses for anguish of spirit, and for cruel bondage.

Exo 6:10 YHWH spoke to Moses, saying,

Exo 6:11 "Go in, speak to Pharaoh king of Egypt, that he let the children of Israel go out of his land."

Exo 6:12 Moses spoke before YHWH, saying, "Behold, the children of Israel haven't listened to me. How then shall Pharaoh listen to me, who am of uncircumcised lips?"

Exo 6:13 YHWH spoke to Moses and to Aaron, and gave them a command to the children of Israel, and to Pharaoh king of Egypt, to bring the children of Israel out of the land of Egypt.

The Genealogy of Moses and Aaron

MONDAY Exo 6:14 These are the heads of their fathers' houses. The sons of Reuben the firstborn of Israel: Hanoch, and Pallu, Hezron, and Carmi; these are the families of Reuben.

Exo 6:15 The sons of Simeon: Jemuel, and Jamin, and Ohad, and Jachin, and Zohar, and Shaul the son of a Canaanite woman; these are the families of Simeon.

Exo 6:16 These are the names of the sons of Levi according to their generations: Gershon, and Kohath, and Merari; and the years of the life of Levi were one hundred thirty-seven years.

Exo 6:17 The sons of Gershon: Libni and Shimei, according to their families.

Exo 6:18 The sons of Kohath: Amram, and Izhar, and Hebron, and Uzziel; and the years of the life of Kohath were one hundred thirty-three years.

Exo 6:19 The sons of Merari: Mahli and Mushi. These are the families of the Levites according to their generations.

Exo 6:20 Amram took Jochebed his father's sister to himself as wife; and she bore him Aaron and Moses: and the years of the life of Amram were a hundred and thirty-seven years.

Exo 6:21 The sons of Izhar: Korah, and Nepheg, and Zichri.

Exo 6:22 The sons of Uzziel: Mishael, and Elzaphan, and Sithri.

Exo 6:23 Aaron took Elisheba, the daughter of Amminadab, the sister of Nahshon, as his wife; and she bore him Nadab and Abihu, Eleazar and Ithamar.

Exo 6:24 The sons of Korah: Assir, and Elkanah, and Abiasaph; these are the families of the Korahites.

Exo 6:25 Eleazar Aaron's son took one of the daughters of Putiel as his wife; and she bore him Phinehas. These are the heads of the fathers' houses of the Levites according to their families.

Exo 6:26 These are that Aaron and Moses, to whom YHWH said, "Bring out the children of Israel from the land of Egypt according to their armies."

Exo 6:27 **These are those who spoke to Pharaoh king of Egypt, to bring out the children of Israel from Egypt. These are that Moses and Aaron.**

Exo 6:28 On the day when YHWH spoke to Moses in the land of Egypt,

TUESDAY Exo 6:29 YHWH spoke to Moses, saying, "I am YHWH. Speak to Pharaoh king of Egypt all that I speak to you."

Exo 6:30 Moses said before YHWH, "Behold, I am of uncircumcised lips, and how shall Pharaoh listen to me?"

Moses and Aaron Before Pharaoh

Exo 7:1 YHWH said to Moses, "Behold, I have made you as God to Pharaoh; and Aaron your brother shall be your prophet.

Exo 7:2 **You shall speak all that I command you; and Aaron your brother shall speak to Pharaoh, that he let the children of Israel go out of his land.**

Exo 7:3 I will harden Pharaoh's heart, and multiply my signs and my wonders in the land of Egypt.

Exo 7:4 But Pharaoh will not listen to you, and I will lay my hand on Egypt, and bring out my armies, my people the children of Israel, out of the land of Egypt by great judgments.

Exo 7:5 The Egyptians shall know that I am YHWH, when I stretch out my hand on Egypt, and bring out the children of Israel from among them."

Exo 7:6 Moses and Aaron did so. As YHWH commanded them, so they did.

Exo 7:7 Moses was eighty years old, and Aaron eighty-three years old, when they spoke to Pharaoh.

WEDNESDAY Exo 7:8 YHWH spoke to Moses and to Aaron, saying,

Exo 7:9 "When Pharaoh speaks to you, saying, 'Perform a miracle!' then you shall tell Aaron, 'Take your rod, and cast it down before Pharaoh, that it become a serpent.'"

Exo 7:10 Moses and Aaron went in to Pharaoh, and they did so, as YHWH had commanded: and Aaron cast down his rod before Pharaoh and before his servants, and it became a serpent.

Exo 7:11 Then Pharaoh also called for the wise men and the sorcerers. They also, the magicians of Egypt, did the same thing with their enchantments.

Exo 7:12 ***For they each cast down their rods, and they became serpents: but Aaron's rod swallowed up their rods.***

Exo 7:13 Pharaoh's heart was hardened, and he didn't listen to them; as YHWH had spoken.

The First Plague: Water Turned to Blood

Exo 7:14 YHWH said to Moses, "Pharaoh's heart is stubborn. He refuses to let the people go.

Exo 7:15 Go to Pharaoh in the morning. Behold, he goes out to the water; and you shall stand by the river's bank to meet him; and the rod which was turned to a serpent you shall take in your hand.

Exo 7:16 You shall tell him, 'YHWH, the God of the Hebrews, has sent me to you, saying, "Let my people go, that they may serve me in the wilderness:" and behold, until now you haven't listened.

Exo 7:17 YHWH says, "In this you shall know that I am YHWH. Behold, I will strike with the rod that is in my hand on the waters which are in the river, and they shall be turned to blood.

Exo 7:18 The fish that are in the river shall die, and the river shall become foul; and the Egyptians shall loathe to drink water from the river."'"

Exo 7:19 YHWH said to Moses, "Tell Aaron, 'Take your rod, and stretch out your hand over the waters of Egypt, over their rivers, over their streams, and over their pools, and over all their ponds of water, that they may become blood; and there shall be blood throughout all the land of Egypt, both in vessels of wood and in vessels of stone.'"

Exo 7:20 Moses and Aaron did so, as YHWH commanded; and he lifted up the rod, and struck the waters that were in the river, in the sight of Pharaoh, and in the sight of his servants; and all the waters that were in the river were turned to blood.

Exo 7:21 The fish that were in the river died; and the river became foul, and the Egyptians couldn't drink water from the river; and the blood was throughout all the land of Egypt.

Exo 7:22 The magicians of Egypt did the same thing with their enchantments; and Pharaoh's heart was hardened, and he didn't listen to them; as YHWH had spoken.

Exo 7:23 Pharaoh turned and went into his house, and he didn't even take this to heart.

Exo 7:24 All the Egyptians dug around the river for water to drink; for they couldn't drink the river water.

Exo 7:25 Seven days were fulfilled, after YHWH had struck the river.

The Second Plague: Frogs

Exo 8:1 **YHWH spoke to Moses, Go in to Pharaoh, and tell him, "This is what YHWH says, 'Let my people go, that they may serve me.**

Exo 8:2 If you refuse to let them go, behold, I will plague all your borders with frogs:

Exo 8:3 and the river shall swarm with frogs, which shall go up and come into your house, and into your bedroom, and on your bed, and into the house of your servants, and on your people, and into your ovens, and into your kneading troughs:

Exo 8:4 and the frogs shall come up both on you, and on your people, and on all your servants.'"

Exo 8:5 YHWH said to Moses, "Tell Aaron, 'Stretch out your hand with your rod over the rivers, over the streams, and over the pools, and cause frogs to come up on the land of Egypt.'"

Exo 8:6 Aaron stretched out his hand over the waters of Egypt; and the frogs came up, and covered the land of Egypt.

THURSDAY Exo 8:7 The magicians did the same thing with their enchantments, and brought up frogs on the land of Egypt.

Exo 8:8 Then Pharaoh called for Moses and Aaron, and said, "Entreat YHWH, that he take away the frogs from me, and from my people; and I will let the people go, that they may sacrifice to YHWH."

Exo 8:9 Moses said to Pharaoh, "I give you the honor of setting the time that I should pray for you, and for your servants, and for your people, that the frogs be destroyed from you and your houses, and remain in the river only."

Exo 8:10 He said, "Tomorrow." He said, "Be it according to your word, that you may know that there is no one like YHWH our God.

Exo 8:11 The frogs shall depart from you, and from your houses, and from your servants, and from your people. They shall remain in the river only."

Exo 8:12 *Moses and Aaron went out from Pharaoh, and Moses cried to YHWH concerning the frogs which he had brought on Pharaoh.*

Exo 8:13 YHWH did according to the word of Moses, and the frogs died out of the houses, out of the courts, and out of the fields.

Exo 8:14 They gathered them together in heaps, and the land stank.

Exo 8:15 But when Pharaoh saw that there was a respite, he hardened his heart, and didn't listen to them, as YHWH had spoken.

The Third Plague: Gnats

Exo 8:16 YHWH said to Moses, "Tell Aaron, 'Stretch out your rod, and strike the dust of the earth, that it may become lice throughout all the land of Egypt.'"

Exo 8:17 They did so; and Aaron stretched out his hand with his rod, and struck the dust of the earth, and there were lice on man, and on animal; all the dust of the earth became lice throughout all the land of Egypt.

Exo 8:18 The magicians tried with their enchantments to produce lice, but they couldn't. There were lice on man, and on animal.

FRIDAY Exo 8:19 *Then the magicians said to Pharaoh, "This is God's finger;" but Pharaoh's heart was hardened, and he didn't listen to them; as YHWH had spoken.*

The Fourth Plague: Flies

Exo 8:20 YHWH said to Moses, "Rise up early in the morning, and stand before Pharaoh; behold, he comes out to the water; and tell him, 'This is what YHWH says, "Let my people go, that they may serve me.

Exo 8:21 Else, if you will not let my people go, behold, I will send swarms of flies on you, and on your servants, and on your people, and into your houses: and the houses of the Egyptians shall be full of swarms of flies, and also the ground whereon they are.

Exo 8:22 I will set apart in that day the land of Goshen, in which my people dwell, that no swarms of flies shall be there; to the end you may know that I am YHWH on the earth.

Exo 8:23 I will put a division between my people and your people: by tomorrow shall this sign be."'"

Exo 8:24 YHWH did so; and there came grievous swarms of flies into the house of Pharaoh, and into his servants' houses: and in all the land of Egypt the land was corrupted by reason of the swarms of flies.

Exo 8:25 Pharaoh called for Moses and for Aaron, and said, "Go, sacrifice to your God in the land!"

Exo 8:26 Moses said, "It isn't appropriate to do so; for we shall sacrifice the abomination of the Egyptians to YHWH our God. Behold, shall we sacrifice the abomination of the Egyptians before their eyes, and won't they stone us?

Exo 8:27 We will go three days' journey into the wilderness, and sacrifice to YHWH our God, as he shall command us."

Exo 8:28 Pharaoh said, "I will let you go, that you may sacrifice to YHWH your God in the wilderness, only you shall not go very far away. Pray for me."

Exo 8:29 Moses said, "Behold, I go out from you, and I will pray to YHWH that the swarms of flies may depart from Pharaoh, from his servants, and from his people, tomorrow; only don't let Pharaoh deal deceitfully any more in not letting the people go to sacrifice to YHWH."

Exo 8:30 Moses went out from Pharaoh, and prayed to YHWH.

Exo 8:31 YHWH did according to the word of Moses, and he removed the swarms of flies from Pharaoh, from his servants, and from his people. There remained not one.

Exo 8:32 Pharaoh hardened his heart this time also, and he didn't let the people go.

The Fifth Plague: Egyptian Livestock Die

Exo 9:1 Then YHWH said to Moses, "Go in to Pharaoh, and tell him, 'This is what YHWH, the God of the Hebrews, says: "Let my people go, that they may serve me.

Exo 9:2 For if you refuse to let them go, and hold them still,

Exo 9:3 behold, YHWH's hand is on your livestock which are in the field, on the horses, on the donkeys, on the camels, on the herds, and on the flocks with a very grievous pestilence.

Exo 9:4 **YHWH will make a distinction between the livestock of Israel and the livestock of Egypt; and nothing shall die of all that belongs to the children of Israel."'"**

Exo 9:5 YHWH appointed a set time, saying, "Tomorrow YHWH shall do this thing in the land."

Exo 9:6 YHWH did that thing on the next day; and all the livestock of Egypt died, but of the livestock of the children of Israel, not one died.

Exo 9:7 Pharaoh sent, and, behold, there was not so much as one of the livestock of the Israelites dead. But the heart of Pharaoh was stubborn, and he didn't let the people go.

The Sixth Plague: Boils

Exo 9:8 YHWH said to Moses and to Aaron, "Take to you handfuls of ashes of the furnace, and let Moses sprinkle it toward the sky in the sight of Pharaoh.

Exo 9:9 It shall become small dust over all the land of Egypt, and shall be a boil breaking out with boils on man and on animal, throughout all the land of Egypt."

Exo 9:10 They took ashes of the furnace, and stood before Pharaoh; and Moses sprinkled it up toward the sky; and it became a boil breaking out with boils on man and on animal.

Exo 9:11 The magicians couldn't stand before Moses because of the boils; for the boils were on the magicians, and on all the Egyptians.

Exo 9:12 YHWH hardened the heart of Pharaoh, and he didn't listen to them, as YHWH had spoken to Moses.

The Seventh Plague: Hail

Exo 9:13 YHWH said to Moses, "Rise up early in the morning, and stand before Pharaoh, and tell him, 'This is what YHWH, the God of the Hebrews, says: "Let my people go, that they may serve me.

Exo 9:14 For this time I will send all my plagues against your heart, against your officials, and against your people; that you may know that there is no one like me in all the earth.

Exo 9:15 For now I would have stretched out my hand, and struck you and your people with pestilence, and you would have been cut off from the earth;

Exo 9:16 but indeed for this cause I have made you stand: to show you my power, and that my name may be declared throughout all the earth;

Exo 9:17 as you still exalt yourself against my people, that you won't let them go.

SABBATH Exo 9:18 Behold, tomorrow about this time I will cause it to rain a very grievous hail, such as has not been in Egypt since the day it was founded even until now.

Exo 9:19 ***Now therefore command that all of your livestock and all that you have in the field be brought into shelter. Every man and animal that is found in the field, and isn't brought home, the hail shall come down on them, and they shall die."'"***

Exo 9:20 Those who feared YHWH's word among the servants of Pharaoh made their servants and their livestock flee into the houses.

Exo 9:21 Whoever didn't respect YHWH's word left his servants and his livestock in the field.

Exo 9:22 YHWH said to Moses, "Stretch out your hand toward the sky, that there may be hail in all the land of Egypt, on man, and on animal, and on every herb of the field, throughout the land of Egypt."

Exo 9:23 Moses stretched out his rod toward the heavens, and YHWH sent thunder, hail, and lightning flashed down to the earth. YHWH rained hail on the land of Egypt.

Exo 9:24 So there was very severe hail, and lightning mixed with the hail, such as had not been in all the land of Egypt since it became a nation.

Exo 9:25 The hail struck throughout all the land of Egypt all that was in the field, both man and animal; and the hail struck every herb of the field, and broke every tree of the field.

Exo 9:26 Only in the land of Goshen, where the children of Israel were, there was no hail.

Exo 9:27 Pharaoh sent, and called for Moses and Aaron, and said to them, "I have sinned this time. YHWH is righteous, and I and my people are wicked.

Exo 9:28 Pray to YHWH; for there has been enough of mighty thunderings and hail. I will let you go, and you shall stay no longer."

Exo 9:29 Moses said to him, "As soon as I have gone out of the city, I will spread abroad my hands to YHWH. The thunders shall cease, and there will not be any more hail; that you may know that the earth is YHWH's.

Exo 9:30 **But as for you and your servants, I know that you don't yet fear YHWH God."**

Exo 9:31 The flax and the barley were struck, for the barley was in the ear, and the flax was in bloom.

Exo 9:32 But the wheat and the spelt were not struck, for they had not grown up.

Exo 9:33 Moses went out of the city from Pharaoh, and spread abroad his hands to YHWH; and the thunders and hail ceased, and the rain was not poured on the earth.

Exo 9:34 When Pharaoh saw that the rain and the hail and the thunders had ceased, he sinned yet more, and hardened his heart, he and his servants.

Exo 9:35 The heart of Pharaoh was hardened, and he didn't let the children of Israel go, just as YHWH had spoken through Moses.

VERSE FIND – EXODUS 7:2

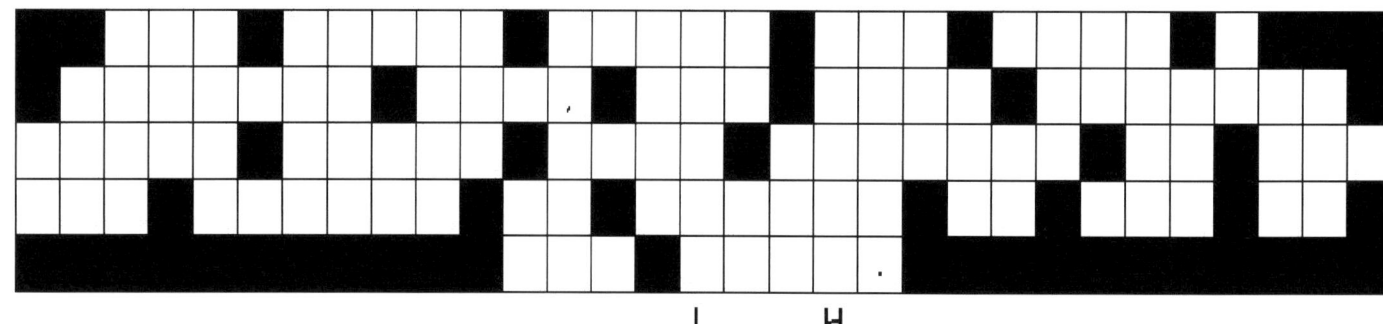

```
                         L    H
   Y  M  S  H   L    T   L A A   D A           T
 A R M P  O D A Y O O S P E S R A Y O R R O H A U O   L E
A H O O U E S H L E L U I S I N K P A L U G O B O T T I O F
T C E O N A N P A L L H F E A L D N E L L A T H R O T H E R T
```

VA'EIRA CROSSWORD

Across
1. There were ten of them
3. Fire and Hail was which plague
4. Swarms of these were the eighth plague
6. when everything is pitch black
8. Infected sores
11. His heart was hardened
12. All of these died

Down
2. Field animals are called this
5. Dust became these (third Plague)
7. Another name for a snake
8. The water turned to this
9. The second plague
10. Moses brother
12. This plague flew in swarms

BO

בֹּא

EXODUS

It Means: **Come!**

Our Fifteenth Torah Portion is called Bo! בֹּא
Exodus 10:1 – Exodus 13:16

PROPHETS: Jeremiah 46:13-28; Ezekiel 20; Joel 2
NEW TESTAMENT: Matthew 26:17-27:66; Luke 2:22-24; John 19:31-37; Acts 13:16-23; Revelation 8:6-9:12, 16:1-21

MAKE A MARK

Each time you hear someone say one of the words below make a '/" beside the word. See how many marks you can get!

heart
plagues
blood
people
hard
Israelites

FIRST FIND

~

If someone mentions a verse or scripture that is NOT in this Torah Portion, see if YOU can be the First to Find it!

The Eighth Plague: Locusts

SUNDAY Exo 10:1 YHWH said to Moses, "Go in to Pharaoh, for I have hardened his heart, and the heart of his servants, that I may show these my signs among them,

Exo 10:2 and that you may tell in the hearing of your son, and of your son's son, what things I have done to Egypt, and my signs which I have done among them; that you may know that I am YHWH."

Exo 10:3 Moses and Aaron went in to Pharaoh, and said to him, "This is what YHWH, the God of the Hebrews, says: 'How long will you refuse to humble yourself before me? Let my people go, that they may serve me.

Exo 10:4 Or else, if you refuse to let my people go, behold, tomorrow I will bring locusts into your country,

Exo 10:5 and they shall cover the surface of the earth, so that one won't be able to see the earth. They shall eat the residue of that which has escaped, which remains to you from the hail, and shall eat every tree which grows for you out of the field.

Exo 10:6 Your houses shall be filled, and the houses of all your servants, and the houses of all the Egyptians; as neither your fathers nor your fathers' fathers have seen, since the day that they were on the earth to this day.'" He turned, and went out from Pharaoh.

Exo 10:7 Pharaoh's servants said to him, "How long will this man be a snare to us? Let the men go, that they may serve YHWH, their God. Don't you yet know that Egypt is destroyed?"

Exo 10:8 **Moses and Aaron were brought again to Pharaoh, and he said to them, "Go, serve YHWH your God; but who are those who will go?"**

Exo 10:9 Moses said, "We will go with our young and with our old; with our sons and with our daughters, with our flocks and with our herds will we go; for we must hold a feast to YHWH."

Exo 10:10 He said to them, "YHWH be with you if I will let you go with your little ones! See, evil is clearly before your faces.

Exo 10:11 Not so! Go now you who are men, and serve YHWH; for that is what you desire!" They were driven out from Pharaoh's presence.

MONDAY Exo 10:12 YHWH said to Moses, "Stretch out your hand over the land of Egypt for the locusts, that they may come up on the land of Egypt, and eat every herb of the land, even all that the hail has left."

Exo 10:13 Moses stretched out his rod over the land of Egypt, and YHWH brought an east wind on the land all that day, and all night; and when it was morning, the east wind brought the locusts.

Exo 10:14 The locusts went up over all the land of Egypt, and rested in all the borders of Egypt. They were very grievous. Before them there were no such locusts as they, nor will there ever be again.

Exo 10:15 For they covered the surface of the whole earth, so that the land was darkened, and they ate every herb of the land, and all the fruit of the trees which the hail had left. There remained nothing green, either tree or herb of the field, through all the land of Egypt.

Exo 10:16 **Then Pharaoh called for Moses and Aaron in haste, and he said, "I have sinned against YHWH your God, and against you.**

Exo 10:17 Now therefore please forgive my sin again, and pray to YHWH your God, that he may also take away from me this death."

Exo 10:18 He went out from Pharaoh, and prayed to YHWH.

Exo 10:19 YHWH turned an exceeding strong west wind, which took up the locusts, and drove them into the Red Sea. There remained not one locust in all the borders of Egypt.

Exo 10:20 But YHWH hardened Pharaoh's heart, and he didn't let the children of Israel go.

The Ninth Plague: Darkness

Exo 10:21 YHWH said to Moses, "Stretch out your hand toward the sky, that there may be darkness over the land of Egypt, even darkness which may be felt."

Exo 10:22 Moses stretched out his hand toward the sky, and there was a thick darkness in all the land of Egypt for three days.

Exo 10:23 They didn't see one another, and nobody rose from his place for three days; but all the children of Israel had light in their dwellings.

TUESDAY Exo 10:24 Pharaoh called to Moses, and said, "Go, serve YHWH. Only let your flocks and your herds stay behind. Let your little ones also go with you."

Exo 10:25 Moses said, "You must also give into our hand sacrifices and burnt offerings, that we may sacrifice to YHWH our God.

Exo 10:26 Our livestock also shall go with us. Not a hoof shall be left behind, for of it we must take to serve YHWH our God; and we don't know with what we must serve YHWH, until we come there."

Exo 10:27 But YHWH hardened Pharaoh's heart, and he wouldn't let them go.

Exo 10:28 **Pharaoh said to him, "Get away from me! Be careful to see my face no more; for in the day you see my face you shall die!"**

Exo 10:29 Moses said, "You have spoken well. I will see your face again no more."

A Final Plague Threatened

Exo 11:1 YHWH said to Moses, "I will bring yet one more plague on Pharaoh, and on Egypt; afterwards he will let you go. When he lets you go, he will surely thrust you out altogether.

Exo 11:2 Speak now in the ears of the people, and let every man ask of his neighbor, and every woman of her neighbor, jewels of silver, and jewels of gold."

Exo 11:3 YHWH gave the people favor in the sight of the Egyptians. Moreover the man Moses was very great in the land of Egypt, in the sight of Pharaoh's servants, and in the sight of the people.

WEDNESDAY Exo 11:4 Moses said, "This is what YHWH says: 'About midnight I will go out into the middle of Egypt,

Exo 11:5 and all the firstborn in the land of Egypt shall die, from the firstborn of Pharaoh who sits on his throne, even to the firstborn of the female servant who is behind the mill; and all the firstborn of livestock.

Exo 11:6 There shall be a great cry throughout all the land of Egypt, such as there has not been, nor shall be any more.

Exo 11:7 ***But against any of the children of Israel a dog won't even bark or move its tongue, against man or animal; that you may know that YHWH makes a distinction between the Egyptians and Israel.***

Exo 11:8 All these servants of yours will come down to me, and bow down themselves to me, saying, "Get out, with all the people who follow you;" and after that I will go out.'" He went out from Pharaoh in hot anger.

Exo 11:9 YHWH said to Moses, "Pharaoh won't listen to you, that my wonders may be multiplied in the land of Egypt."

Exo 11:10 Moses and Aaron did all these wonders before Pharaoh, and YHWH hardened Pharaoh's heart, and he didn't let the children of Israel go out of his land.

The Passover

Exo 12:1 YHWH spoke to Moses and Aaron in the land of Egypt, saying,

Exo 12:2 "This month shall be to you the beginning of months. It shall be the first month of the year to you.

Exo 12:3 Speak to all the congregation of Israel, saying, 'On the tenth day of this month, they shall take to them every man a lamb, according to their fathers' houses, a lamb for a household;

Exo 12:4 and if the household is too little for a lamb, then he and his neighbor next to his house shall take one according to the number of the souls; according to what everyone can eat you shall make your count for the lamb.

Exo 12:5 Your lamb shall be without defect, a male a year old. You shall take it from the sheep, or from the goats:

Exo 12:6 and you shall keep it until the fourteenth day of the same month; and the whole assembly of the congregation of Israel shall kill it at evening.

Exo 12:7 They shall take some of the blood, and put it on the two door posts and on the lintel, on the houses in which they shall eat it.

Exo 12:8 They shall eat the meat in that night, roasted with fire, and unleavened bread. They shall eat it with bitter herbs.

Exo 12:9 Don't eat it raw, nor boiled at all with water, but roasted with fire; with its head, its legs and its inner parts.

Exo 12:10 You shall let nothing of it remain until the morning; but that which remains of it until the morning you shall burn with fire.

Exo 12:11 This is how you shall eat it: with your belt on your waist, your shoes on your feet, and your staff in your hand; and you shall eat it in haste: it is YHWH's Passover.

Exo 12:12 For I will go through the land of Egypt in that night, and will strike all the firstborn in the land of Egypt, both man and animal. Against all the gods of Egypt I will execute judgments: I am YHWH.

Exo 12:13 The blood shall be to you for a token on the houses where you are: and when I see the blood, I will pass over you, and there shall no plague be on you to destroy you, when I strike the land of Egypt.

Exo 12:14 This day shall be to you for a memorial, and you shall keep it a feast to YHWH: throughout your generations you shall keep it a feast by an ordinance forever.

Exo 12:15 "'Seven days you shall eat unleavened bread; even the first day you shall put away yeast out of your houses, for whoever eats leavened bread from the first day until the seventh day, that soul shall be cut off from Israel.

Exo 12:16 In the first day there shall be to you a holy convocation, and in the seventh day a holy convocation; no kind of work shall be done in them, except that which every man must eat, that only may be done by you.

Exo 12:17 You shall observe the feast of unleavened bread; for in this same day I have brought your armies out of the land of Egypt: therefore you shall observe this day throughout your generations by an ordinance forever.

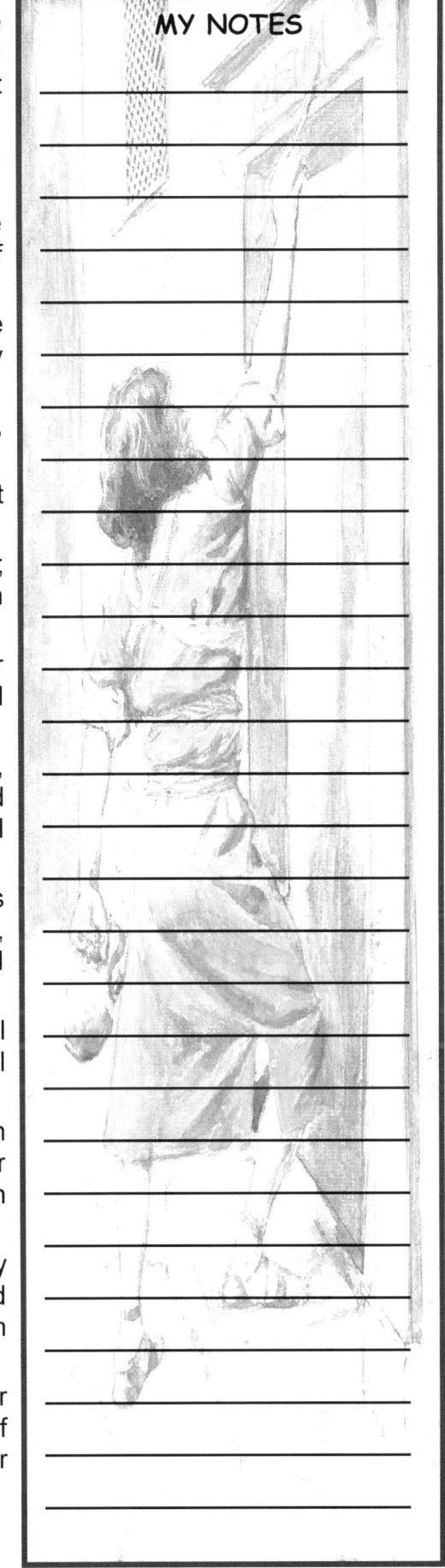

MY NOTES

Exo 12:18 *In the first month, on the fourteenth day of the month at evening, you shall eat unleavened bread, until the twenty first day of the month at evening.*

Exo 12:19 There shall be no yeast found in your houses for seven days, for whoever eats that which is leavened, that soul shall be cut off from the congregation of Israel, whether he is a foreigner, or one who is born in the land.

Exo 12:20 You shall eat nothing leavened. In all your habitations you shall eat unleavened bread.'"

THURSDAY Exo 12:21 Then Moses called for all the elders of Israel, and said to them, "Draw out, and take lambs according to your families, and kill the Passover.

Exo 12:22 You shall take a bunch of hyssop, and dip it in the blood that is in the basin, and strike the lintel and the two door posts with the blood that is in the basin; and none of you shall go out of the door of his house until the morning.

Exo 12:23 For YHWH will pass through to strike the Egyptians; and when he sees the blood on the lintel, and on the two door posts, YHWH will pass over the door, and will not allow the destroyer to come in to your houses to strike you.

Exo 12:24 You shall observe this thing for an ordinance to you and to your sons forever.

Exo 12:25 It shall happen when you have come to the land which YHWH will give you, according as he has promised, that you shall keep this service.

Exo 12:26 It will happen, when your children ask you, 'What do you mean by this service?'

Exo 12:27 that you shall say, 'It is the sacrifice of YHWH's Passover, who passed over the houses of the children of Israel in Egypt, when he struck the Egyptians, and spared our houses.'" The people bowed their heads and worshiped.

Exo 12:28 *The children of Israel went and did so; as YHWH had commanded Moses and Aaron, so they did.*

The Tenth Plague: Death of the Firstborn

FRIDAY Exo 12:29 At midnight, YHWH struck all the firstborn in the land of Egypt, from the firstborn of Pharaoh who sat on his throne to the firstborn of the captive who was in the dungeon; and all the firstborn of livestock.

Exo 12:30 Pharaoh rose up in the night, he, and all his servants, and all the Egyptians; and there was a great cry in Egypt, for there was not a house where there was not one dead.

Exo 12:31 He called for Moses and Aaron by night, and said, "Rise up, get out from among my people, both you and the children of Israel; and go, serve YHWH, as you have said!

Exo 12:32 Take both your flocks and your herds, as you have said, and be gone; and bless me also!"

page 38

The Exodus

Exo 12:33 The Egyptians were urgent with the people, to send them out of the land in haste, for they said, "We are all dead men."

Exo 12:34 The people took their dough before it was leavened, their kneading troughs being bound up in their clothes on their shoulders.

Exo 12:35 The children of Israel did according to the word of Moses; and they asked of the Egyptians jewels of silver, and jewels of gold, and clothing.

Exo 12:36 **YHWH gave the people favor in the sight of the Egyptians, so that they let them have what they asked. They plundered the Egyptians.**

Exo 12:37 The children of Israel traveled from Rameses to Succoth, about six hundred thousand on foot who were men, in addition to children.

Exo 12:38 A mixed multitude went up also with them, with flocks, herds, and even very much livestock.

Exo 12:39 They baked unleavened cakes of the dough which they brought out of Egypt; for it wasn't leavened, because they were thrust out of Egypt, and couldn't wait, and they had not prepared any food for themselves.

Exo 12:40 Now the time that the children of Israel lived in Egypt was four hundred thirty years.

Exo 12:41 At the end of four hundred thirty years, to the day, all of YHWH's armies went out from the land of Egypt.

Exo 12:42 It is a night to be much observed to YHWH for bringing them out from the land of Egypt. This is that night of YHWH, to be much observed of all the children of Israel throughout their generations.

Institution of the Passover

Exo 12:43 YHWH said to Moses and Aaron, "This is the ordinance of the Passover. No foreigner shall eat of it,

Exo 12:44 but every man's servant who is bought for money, when you have circumcised him, then shall he eat of it.

Exo 12:45 A foreigner and a hired servant shall not eat of it.

Exo 12:46 It must be eaten in one house. You shall not carry any of the meat outside of the house. Do not break any of its bones.

Exo 12:47 All the congregation of Israel shall keep it.

Exo 12:48 When a stranger shall live as a foreigner with you, and will keep the Passover to YHWH, let all his males be circumcised, and then let him come near and keep it; and he shall be as one who is born in the land: but no uncircumcised person shall eat of it.

Exo 12:49 One law shall be to him who is born at home, and to the stranger who lives as a foreigner among you."

Exo 12:50 All the children of Israel did so. As YHWH commanded Moses and Aaron, so they did.

Exo 12:51 That same day, YHWH brought the children of Israel out of the land of Egypt by their armies.

Consecration of the Firstborn

<u>SABBATH</u> Exo 13:1 YHWH spoke to Moses, saying,

Exo 13:2 "Sanctify to me all the firstborn, whatever opens the womb among the children of Israel, both of man and of animal. It is mine."

The Feast of Unleavened Bread

Exo 13:3 Moses said to the people, "Remember this day, in which you came out of Egypt, out of the house of bondage; for by strength of hand YHWH brought you out from this place. No leavened bread shall be eaten.

Exo 13:4 Today you go out in the month Abib.

Exo 13:5 It shall be, when YHWH shall bring you into the land of the Canaanite, and the Hittite, and the Amorite, and the Hivite, and the Jebusite, which he swore to your fathers to give you, a land flowing with milk and honey, that you shall keep this service in this month.

Exo 13:6 **Seven days you shall eat unleavened bread, and in the seventh day shall be a feast to YHWH.**

Exo 13:7 Unleavened bread shall be eaten throughout the seven days; and no leavened bread shall be seen with you. No yeast shall be seen with you, within all your borders.

Exo 13:8 You shall tell your son in that day, saying, 'It is because of that which YHWH did for me when I came out of Egypt.'

Exo 13:9 It shall be for a sign to you on your hand, and for a memorial between your eyes, that YHWH's law may be in your mouth; for with a strong hand YHWH has brought you out of Egypt.

Exo 13:10 You shall therefore keep this ordinance in its season from year to year.

Exo 13:11 "It shall be, when YHWH shall bring you into the land of the Canaanite, as he swore to you and to your fathers, and shall give it you,

Exo 13:12 that you shall set apart to YHWH all that opens the womb, and every firstborn that comes from an animal which you have. The males shall be YHWH's.

Exo 13:13 Every firstborn of a donkey you shall redeem with a lamb; and if you will not redeem it, then you shall break its neck; and you shall redeem all the firstborn of man among your sons.

Exo 13:14 It shall be, when your son asks you in time to come, saying, 'What is this?' that you shall tell him, 'By strength of hand YHWH brought us out from Egypt, from the house of bondage.

Exo 13:15 When Pharaoh stubbornly refused to let us go, YHWH killed all the firstborn in the land of Egypt, both the firstborn of man, and the firstborn of livestock. Therefore I sacrifice to YHWH all that opens the womb, being males; but all the firstborn of my sons I redeem.'

Exo 13:16 It shall be for a sign on your hand, and for symbols between your eyes: for by strength of hand YHWH brought us out of Egypt."

MY NOTES

VERSE FIND – EXODUS 10:1

PASSOVER MAZE

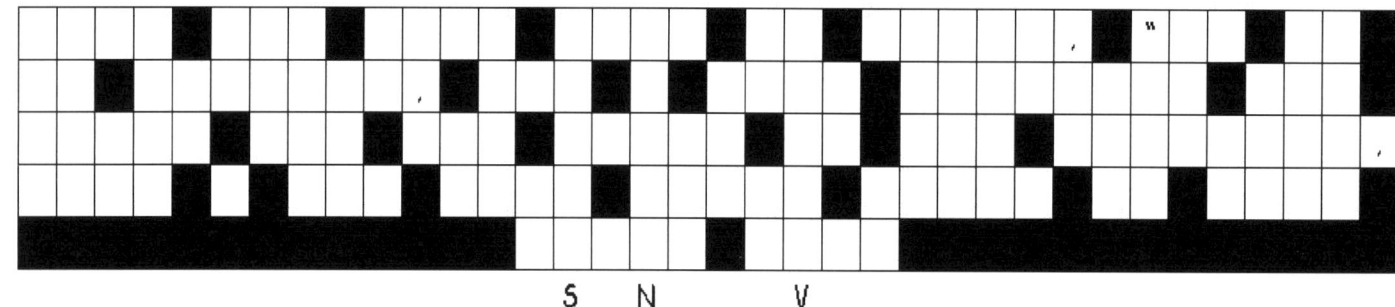

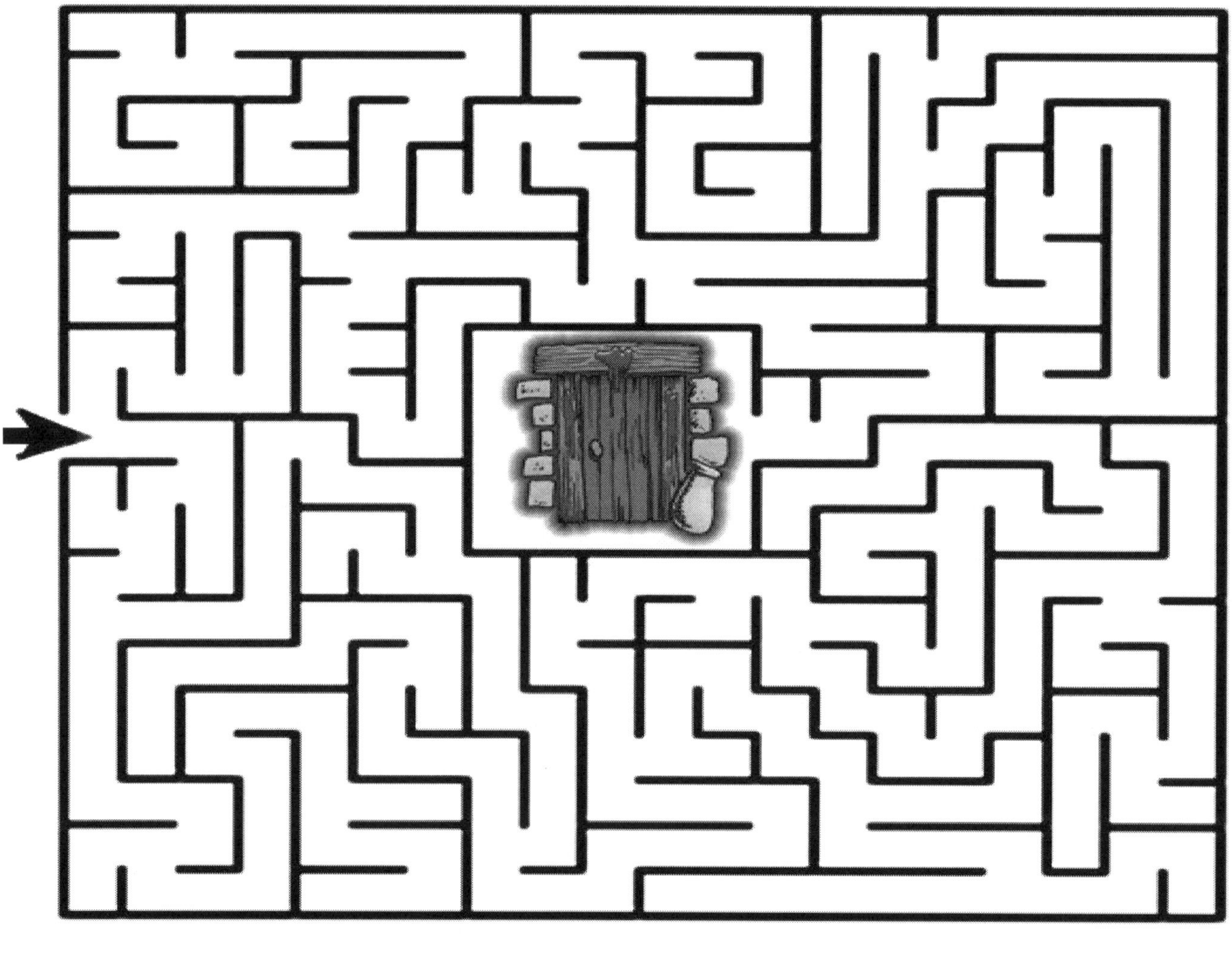

BO WORDFIND

```
Q R E O X W R I F O L E N X W
S L E F S L E I L A U P Z D Q
O T V V I M R D I U L G T K D
A D A N O S D R V N D S Q U O
D J T T T S O P N L A A N W O
R E Z B U M S C I E A Y E N L
L H O L E T Y A F A N Y D R B
D R O M L U E M P V A L A M B
N E U G A L P O M E I H V H Q
S T S O P R O O D N T Y U L D
C O V E N A N T F E P S B C A
J S E D I W U H A D Y S P G Z
W O I H U O Z N T U G O I R B
X W L M R A F A Q N E P T N F
T I C X T G X X Q J L R J C Q
```

BLOOD	BREAD	COVENANT
DOORPOSTS	EGYPTIAN	FEAST
FIRSTBORN	HYSSOP	LAMB
LINTEL	MEMORIAL	PASSOVER
PLAGUE	STATUTE	UNLEAVENED

BESHAIACH
בְּשַׁלַח
EXODUS

It Means: **When he sent out**

Our Sixteenth Torah Portion is called Beshaiach! בְּשַׁלַח
Exodus 13:17 – Exodus 17:16

PROPHETS: Judges 4:4-5:31
NEW TESTAMENT: John 6:25-35, 19:31-37; Romans 6:1-23; 1 Corinthians 10:1-13; 2 Corinthians 8:1-15; Revelation 15:1-4

MAKE A MARK

Each time you hear someone say one of the words below make a '*/*" beside the word. See how many marks you can get!

heart	
plagues	
blood	
people	
hard	
Israelites	

FIRST FIND

~

If someone mentions a verse or scripture that is NOT in this Torah Portion, see if YOU can be the First to Find it!

Pillars of Cloud and Fire

SUNDAY Exo 13:17 When Pharaoh had let the people go, God didn't lead them by the way of the land of the Philistines, although that was near; for God said, "Lest perhaps the people change their minds when they see war, and they return to Egypt";

Exo 13:18 but God led the people around by the way of the wilderness by the Red Sea; and the children of Israel went up armed out of the land of Egypt.

Exo 13:19 Moses took the bones of Joseph with him, for he had made the children of Israel swear, saying, "God will surely visit you, and you shall carry up my bones away from here with you."

Exo 13:20 They took their journey from Succoth, and encamped in Etham, in the edge of the wilderness.

Exo 13:21 **YHWH went before them by day in a pillar of cloud, to lead them on their way, and by night in a pillar of fire, to give them light, that they might go by day and by night:**

Exo 13:22 the pillar of cloud by day, and the pillar of fire by night, didn't depart from before the people.

Crossing the Red Sea

Exo 14:1 YHWH spoke to Moses, saying,

Exo 14:2 "Speak to the children of Israel, that they turn back and encamp before Pihahiroth, between Migdol and the sea, before Baal Zephon. You shall encamp opposite it by the sea.

Exo 14:3 Pharaoh will say of the children of Israel, 'They are entangled in the land. The wilderness has shut them in.'

Exo 14:4 I will harden Pharaoh's heart, and he will follow after them; and I will get honor over Pharaoh, and over all his armies; and the Egyptians shall know that I am YHWH." They did so.

Exo 14:5 The king of Egypt was told that the people had fled; and the heart of Pharaoh and of his servants was changed towards the people, and they said, "What is this we have done, that we have let Israel go from serving us?"

Exo 14:6 He prepared his chariot, and took his army with him;

Exo 14:7 and he took six hundred chosen chariots, and all the chariots of Egypt, and captains over all of them.

Exo 14:8 YHWH hardened the heart of Pharaoh king of Egypt, and he pursued the children of Israel; for the children of Israel went out with a high hand.

MONDAY Exo 14:9 The Egyptians pursued them. All the horses and chariots of Pharaoh, his horsemen, and his army overtook them encamping by the sea, beside Pihahiroth, before Baal Zephon.

Exo 14:10 When Pharaoh came near, the children of Israel lifted up their eyes, and behold, the Egyptians were marching after them; and they were very afraid. The children of Israel cried out to YHWH.

Exo 14:11 They said to Moses, "Because there were no graves in Egypt, have you taken us away to die in the wilderness? Why have you treated us this way, to bring us out of Egypt?

Exo 14:12 Isn't this the word that we spoke to you in Egypt, saying, 'Leave us alone, that we may serve the Egyptians?' For it would have been better for us to serve the Egyptians than to die in the wilderness."

Exo 14:13 **Moses said to the people, "Don't be afraid. Stand still, and see the salvation of YHWH, which he will work for you today: for the Egyptians whom you have seen today, you shall never see them again.**

Exo 14:14 YHWH will fight for you, and you shall be still."

TUESDAY Exo 14:15 YHWH said to Moses, "Why do you cry to me? Speak to the children of Israel, that they go forward.

Exo 14:16 Lift up your rod, and stretch out your hand over the sea, and divide it: and the children of Israel shall go into the middle of the sea on dry ground.

Exo 14:17 Behold, I myself will harden the hearts of the Egyptians, and they shall go in after them: and I will get myself honor over Pharaoh, and over all his armies, over his chariots, and over his horsemen.

Exo 14:18 **The Egyptians shall know that I am YHWH, when I have gotten myself honor over Pharaoh, over his chariots, and over his horsemen."**

Exo 14:19 The angel of God, who went before the camp of Israel, moved and went behind them; and the pillar of cloud moved from before them, and stood behind them.

Exo 14:20 It came between the camp of Egypt and the camp of Israel; and there was the cloud and the darkness, yet gave it light by night: and one didn't come near the other all night.

Exo 14:21 Moses stretched out his hand over the sea, and YHWH caused the sea to go back by a strong east wind all night, and made the sea dry land, and the waters were divided.

Exo 14:22 The children of Israel went into the middle of the sea on the dry ground, and the waters were a wall to them on their right hand, and on their left.

Exo 14:23 The Egyptians pursued, and went in after them into the middle of the sea: all of Pharaoh's horses, his chariots, and his horsemen.

Exo 14:24 In the morning watch, YHWH looked out on the Egyptian army through the pillar of fire and of cloud, and confused the Egyptian army.

Exo 14:25 He took off their chariot wheels, and they drove them heavily; so that the Egyptians said, "Let's flee from the face of Israel, for YHWH fights for them against the Egyptians!"

WEDNESDAY Exo 14:26 YHWH said to Moses, "Stretch out your hand over the sea, that the waters may come again on the Egyptians, on their chariots, and on their horsemen."

Exo 14:27 Moses stretched out his hand over the sea, and the sea returned to its strength when the morning appeared; and the Egyptians fled against it. YHWH overthrew the Egyptians in the middle of the sea.

Exo 14:28 The waters returned, and covered the chariots and the horsemen, even all Pharaoh's army that went in after them into the sea. There remained not so much as one of them.

Exo 14:29 But the children of Israel walked on dry land in the middle of the sea, and the waters were a wall to them on their right hand, and on their left.

Exo 14:30 Thus YHWH saved Israel that day out of the hand of the Egyptians; and Israel saw the Egyptians dead on the seashore.

Exo 14:31 Israel saw the great work which YHWH did to the Egyptians, and the people feared YHWH; and they believed in YHWH, and in his servant Moses.

The Song of Moses

Exo 15:1 Then Moses and the children of Israel sang this song to YHWH, and said, "I will sing to YHWH, for he has triumphed gloriously. The horse and his rider he has thrown into the sea.

Exo 15:2 ***Yah is my strength and song. He has become my salvation. This is my God, and I will praise him; my father's God, and I will exalt him.***

Exo 15:3 YHWH is a man of war. YHWH is his name.

Exo 15:4 He has cast Pharaoh's chariots and his army into the sea. His chosen captains are sunk in the Red Sea.

Exo 15:5 The deeps cover them. They went down into the depths like a stone.

Exo 15:6 Your right hand, YHWH, is glorious in power. Your right hand, YHWH, dashes the enemy in pieces.

Exo 15:7 In the greatness of your excellency, you overthrow those who rise up against you. You send out your wrath. It consumes them as stubble.

Exo 15:8 With the blast of your nostrils, the waters were piled up. The floods stood upright as a heap. The deeps were congealed in the heart of the sea.

Exo 15:9 The enemy said, 'I will pursue. I will overtake. I will divide the plunder. My desire shall be satisfied on them. I will draw my sword, my hand shall destroy them.'

Exo 15:10 You blew with your wind. The sea covered them. They sank like lead in the mighty waters.

Exo 15:11 Who is like you, YHWH, among the gods? Who is like you, glorious in holiness, fearful in praises, doing wonders?

Exo 15:12 You stretched out your right hand. The earth swallowed them.

Exo 15:13 "You, in your loving kindness, have led the people that you have redeemed. You have guided them in your strength to your holy habitation.

Exo 15:14 The peoples have heard. They tremble. Pangs have taken hold on the inhabitants of Philistia.

Exo 15:15 Then the chiefs of Edom were dismayed. Trembling takes hold of the mighty men of Moab. All the inhabitants of Canaan have melted away.

Exo 15:16 Terror and dread falls on them. By the greatness of your arm they are as still as a stone— until your people pass over, YHWH, until the people you have purchased pass over.

Exo 15:17 You shall bring them in, and plant them in the mountain of your inheritance, the place, YHWH, which you have made for yourself to dwell in; the sanctuary, Lord, which your hands have established.

Exo 15:18 YHWH shall reign forever and ever."

Exo 15:19 For the horses of Pharaoh went in with his chariots and with his horsemen into the sea, and YHWH brought back the waters of the sea on them; but the children of Israel walked on dry land in the middle of the sea.

Exo 15:20 Miriam the prophetess, the sister of Aaron, took a tambourine in her hand; and all the women went out after her with tambourines and with dances.

Exo 15:21 Miriam answered them, "Sing to YHWH, for he has triumphed gloriously. The horse and his rider he has thrown into the sea."

Bitter Water Made Sweet

Exo 15:22 Moses led Israel onward from the Red Sea, and they went out into the wilderness of Shur; and they went three days in the wilderness, and found no water.

Exo 15:23 When they came to Marah, they couldn't drink from the waters of Marah, for they were bitter. Therefore its name was called Marah.

Exo 15:24 The people murmured against Moses, saying, "What shall we drink?"

Exo 15:25 Then he cried to YHWH. YHWH showed him a tree, and he threw it into the waters, and the waters were made sweet. There he made a statute and an ordinance for them, and there he tested them;

Exo 15:26 *and he said, "If you will diligently listen to YHWH your God's voice, and will do that which is right in his eyes, and will pay attention to his commandments, and keep all his statutes, I will put none of the diseases on you, which I have put on the Egyptians; for I am YHWH who heals you."*

THURSDAY Exo 15:27 They came to Elim, where there were twelve springs of water, and seventy palm trees: and they encamped there by the waters.

Bread from Heaven

Exo 16:1 They took their journey from Elim, and all the congregation of the children of Israel came to the wilderness of Sin, which is between Elim and Sinai, on the fifteenth day of the second month after their departing out of the land of Egypt.

Exo 16:2 The whole congregation of the children of Israel murmured against Moses and against Aaron in the wilderness;

Exo 16:3 and the children of Israel said to them, "We wish that we had died by YHWH's hand in the land of Egypt, when we sat by the meat pots, when we ate our fill of bread, for you have brought us out into this wilderness, to kill this whole assembly with hunger."

Exo 16:4 Then YHWH said to Moses, "Behold, I will rain bread from the sky for you, and the people shall go out and gather a day's portion every day, that I may test them, whether they will walk in my law, or not.

Exo 16:5 It shall come to pass on the sixth day, that they shall prepare that which they bring in, and it shall be twice as much as they gather daily."

Exo 16:6 Moses and Aaron said to all the children of Israel, "At evening, then you shall know that YHWH has brought you out from the land of Egypt;

Exo 16:7 and in the morning, then you shall see YHWH's glory; because he hears your murmurings against YHWH. Who are we, that you murmur against us?"

Exo 16:8 *Moses said, "Now YHWH shall give you meat to eat in the evening, and in the morning bread to satisfy you; because YHWH hears your murmurings which you murmur against him. And who are we? Your murmurings are not against us, but against YHWH."*

Exo 16:9 Moses said to Aaron, "Tell all the congregation of the children of Israel, 'Come near before YHWH, for he has heard your murmurings.'"

Exo 16:10 As Aaron spoke to the whole congregation of the children of Israel, they looked toward the wilderness, and behold, YHWH's glory appeared in the cloud.

FRIDAY Exo 16:11 YHWH spoke to Moses, saying,

Exo 16:12 "I have heard the murmurings of the children of Israel. Speak to them, saying, 'At evening you shall eat meat, and in the morning you shall be filled with bread: and you shall know that I am YHWH your God.'"

Exo 16:13 In the evening, quail came up and covered the camp; and in the morning the dew lay around the camp.

Exo 16:14 When the dew that lay had gone, behold, on the surface of the wilderness was a small round thing, small as the frost on the ground.

Exo 16:15 When the children of Israel saw it, they said to one another, "What is it?" For they didn't know what it was. Moses said to them, "It is the bread which YHWH has given you to eat."

Exo 16:16 This is the thing which YHWH has commanded: "Gather of it everyone according to his eating; an omer a head, according to the number of your persons, you shall take it, every man for those who are in his tent."

Exo 16:17 The children of Israel did so, and gathered some more, some less.

Exo 16:18 When they measured it with an omer, he who gathered much had nothing over, and he who gathered little had no lack. They gathered every man according to his eating.

Exo 16:19 Moses said to them, "Let no one leave of it until the morning."

Exo 16:20 Notwithstanding they didn't listen to Moses, but some of them left of it until the morning, and it bred worms, and became foul: and Moses was angry with them.

Exo 16:21 They gathered it morning by morning, everyone according to his eating. When the sun grew hot, it melted.

Exo 16:22 On the sixth day, they gathered twice as much bread, two omers for each one, and all the rulers of the congregation came and told Moses.

Exo 16:23 He said to them, "This is that which YHWH has spoken, 'Tomorrow is a solemn rest, a holy Sabbath to YHWH. Bake that which you want to bake, and boil that which you want to boil; and all that remains over lay up for yourselves to be kept until the morning.'"

Exo 16:24 They laid it up until the morning, as Moses asked, and it didn't become foul, and there were no worms in it.

Exo 16:25 Moses said, "Eat that today, for today is a Sabbath to YHWH. Today you shall not find it in the field.

Exo 16:26 Six days you shall gather it, but on the seventh day is the Sabbath. In it there shall be none."

Exo 16:27 On the seventh day, some of the people went out to gather, and they found none.

Exo 16:28 YHWH said to Moses, "How long do you refuse to keep my commandments and my laws?

Exo 16:29 Behold, because YHWH has given you the Sabbath, therefore he gives you on the sixth day the bread of two days. Everyone stay in his place. Let no one go out of his place on the seventh day."

Exo 16:30 So the people rested on the seventh day.

Exo 16:31 The house of Israel called its name Manna, and it was like coriander seed, white; and its taste was like wafers with honey.

Exo 16:32 Moses said, "This is the thing which YHWH has commanded, 'Let an omer-full of it be kept throughout your generations, that they may see the bread with which I fed you in the wilderness, when I brought you out of the land of Egypt.'"

Exo 16:33 Moses said to Aaron, "Take a pot, and put an omer-full of manna in it, and lay it up before YHWH, to be kept throughout your generations."

Exo 16:34 As YHWH commanded Moses, so Aaron laid it up before the Testimony, to be kept.

Exo 16:35 **The children of Israel ate the manna forty years, until they came to an inhabited land. They ate the manna until they came to the borders of the land of Canaan.**

Exo 16:36 Now an omer is one tenth of an ephah.

Water from the Rock

<u>SABBATH</u> Exo 17:1 All the congregation of the children of Israel traveled from the wilderness of Sin, by their journeys, according to YHWH's commandment, and encamped in Rephidim; but there was no water for the people to drink.

Exo 17:2 Therefore the people quarreled with Moses, and said, "Give us water to drink." Moses said to them, "Why do you quarrel with me? Why do you test YHWH?"

Exo 17:3 The people were thirsty for water there; and the people murmured against Moses, and said, "Why have you brought us up out of Egypt, to kill us, our children, and our livestock with thirst?"

Exo 17:4 Moses cried to YHWH, saying, "What shall I do with these people? They are almost ready to stone me."

Exo 17:5 YHWH said to Moses, "Walk on before the people, and take the elders of Israel with you, and take the rod in your hand with which you struck the Nile, and go.

Exo 17:6 Behold, I will stand before you there on the rock in Horeb. You shall strike the rock, and water will come out of it, that the people may drink." Moses did so in the sight of the elders of Israel.

Exo 17:7 He called the name of the place Massah, and Meribah, because the children of Israel quarreled, and because they tested YHWH, saying, "Is YHWH among us, or not?"

Israel Defeats Amalek

Exo 17:8 Then Amalek came and fought with Israel in Rephidim.

Exo 17:9 Moses said to Joshua, "Choose men for us, and go out, fight with Amalek. Tomorrow I will stand on the top of the hill with God's rod in my hand."

Exo 17:10 So Joshua did as Moses had told him, and fought with Amalek; and Moses, Aaron, and Hur went up to the top of the hill.

Exo 17:11 When Moses held up his hand, Israel prevailed. When he let down his hand, Amalek prevailed.

Exo 17:12 But Moses' hands were heavy; and they took a stone, and put it under him, and he sat on it. Aaron and Hur held up his hands, the one on the one side, and the other on the other side. His hands were steady until sunset.

Exo 17:13 Joshua defeated Amalek and his people with the edge of the sword.

Exo 17:14 **YHWH said to Moses, "Write this for a memorial in a book, and rehearse it in the ears of Joshua: that I will utterly blot out the memory of Amalek from under the sky."**

Exo 17:15 Moses built an altar, and called its name YHWH our Banner.

Exo 17:16 He said, "Yah has sworn: 'YHWH will have war with Amalek from generation to generation.'"

LETTER TILES – EXODUS 13:21

E	T	ORE	IVE	T	T	RAV	, AT	. Y	N
BY	WAY	IGH	AND	LE	DAY	M	A	LON
AD	THAT	WE	A	EL	NT	EM
TH	LIG	TO	G	AN	G T	THE	BY
FIR	E L	BY	DAY	Y M	PIL	IGH	HT
IN	IN	OUD	ILL	OF	A P	HE	NIG
EM	TH	OF	TH	ORD	HT ,	THE	ND
BEF	D B	CL	AR	LAR

CRYPTOGRAM – EXODUS 14:21

A	B	C	D	E	F	G	H	I	J	K	L	M	N	O	P	Q	R	S	T	U	V	W	X	Y	Z
26														3				22							

page 55

YITRO

יִתְרוֹ

EXODUS

It Means: **Jethro**

Our Seventeenth Torah Portion is called Yitro! יִתְרוֹ
Exodus 18:1 – Exodus 20:23

PROPHETS: Isaiah 6:1-7:6; 9:2-7
NEW TESTAMENT: Matthew 5:1-48, 5:1-11,19:16-30; Acts 6:1-7; Romans 2:10-29,7:1-8-15;13:8-10; Ephesians 6:1-3; 1 Timothy 3:1-14;2 Timothy 2:2; Titus 1:5-9; Hebrews 8:10; 12:18-29; James 2:8-13; 1 Peter 2:9-10; 1 John 2-5; Revelation 12:10-17

MAKE A MARK

Each time you hear someone say one of the words below make a '/" beside the word. See how many marks you can get!

heart	
plagues	
blood	
people	
hard	
Israelites	

FIRST FIND

~

If someone mentions a verse or scripture that is NOT in this Torah Portion, see if YOU can be the First to Find it!

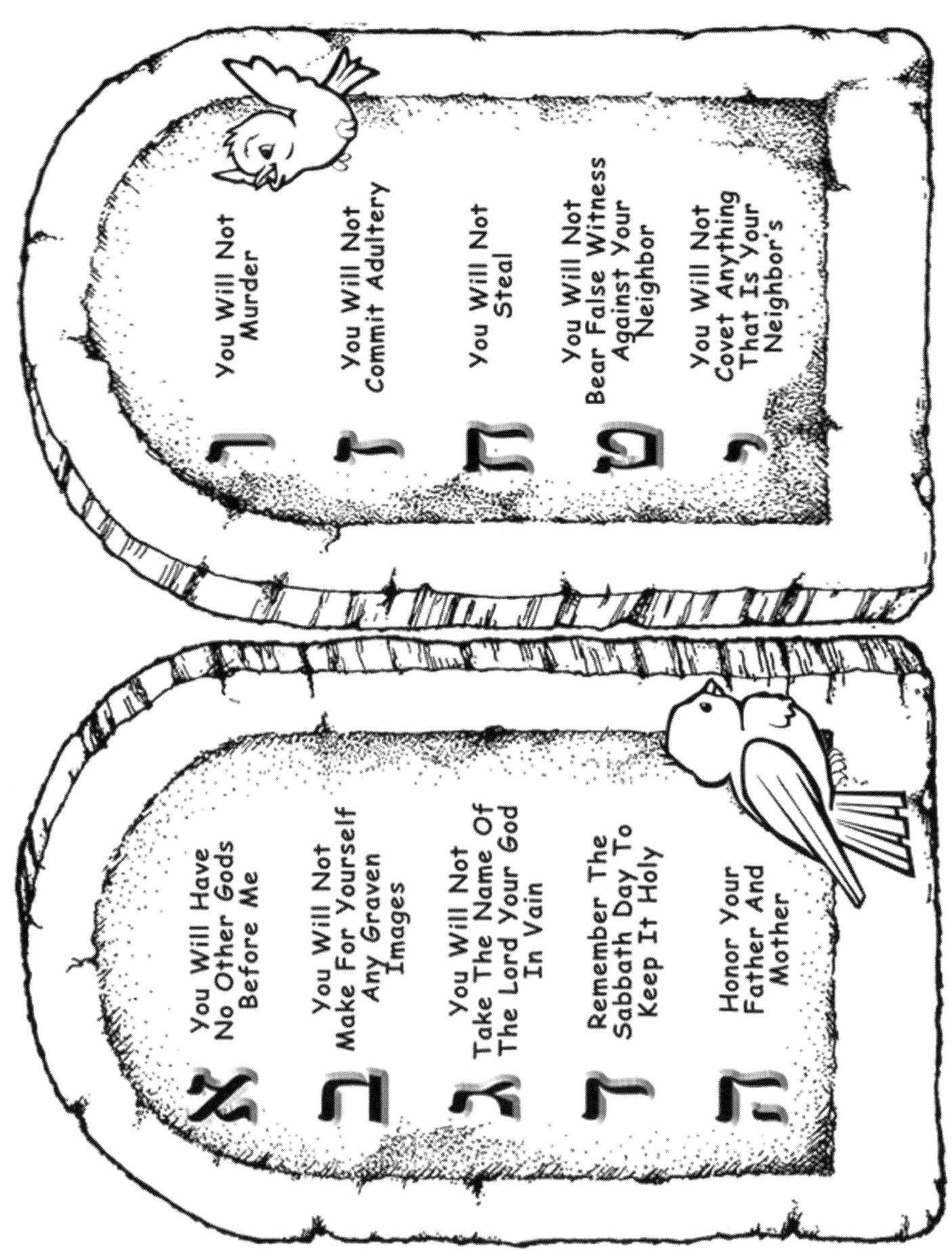

Jethro's Advice

SUNDAY Exo 18:1 Now Jethro, the priest of Midian, Moses' father-in-law, heard of all that God had done for Moses, and for Israel his people, how that YHWH had brought Israel out of Egypt.

Exo 18:2 Jethro, Moses' father-in-law, received Zipporah, Moses' wife, after he had sent her away,

Exo 18:3 and her two sons. The name of one son was Gershom, for Moses said, "I have lived as a foreigner in a foreign land".

Exo 18:4 The name of the other was Eliezer, for he said, "My father's God was my help and delivered me from Pharaoh's sword."

Exo 18:5 Jethro, Moses' father-in-law, came with his sons and his wife to Moses into the wilderness where he was encamped, at the Mountain of God.

Exo 18:6 He said to Moses, "I, your father-in-law Jethro, have come to you with your wife, and her two sons with her."

Exo 18:7 Moses went out to meet his father-in-law, and bowed and kissed him. They asked each other of their welfare, and they came into the tent.

Exo 18:8 Moses told his father-in-law all that YHWH had done to Pharaoh and to the Egyptians for Israel's sake, all the hardships that had come on them on the way, and how YHWH delivered them.

Exo 18:9 Jethro rejoiced for all the goodness which YHWH had done to Israel, in that he had delivered them out of the hand of the Egyptians.

Exo 18:10 *Jethro said, "Blessed be YHWH, who has delivered you out of the hand of the Egyptians, and out of the hand of Pharaoh; who has delivered the people from under the hand of the Egyptians.*

Exo 18:11 Now I know that YHWH is greater than all gods because of the thing in which they dealt arrogantly against them."

Exo 18:12 Jethro, Moses' father-in-law, took a burnt offering and sacrifices for God. Aaron came with all the elders of Israel, to eat bread with Moses' father-in-law before God.

MONDAY Exo 18:13 On the next day, Moses sat to judge the people, and the people stood around Moses from the morning to the evening.

Exo 18:14 When Moses' father-in-law saw all that he did to the people, he said, "What is this thing that you do for the people? Why do you sit alone, and all the people stand around you from morning to evening?"

Exo 18:15 Moses said to his father-in-law, "Because the people come to me to inquire of God.

Exo 18:16 When they have a matter, they come to me, and I judge between a man and his neighbor, and I make them know the statutes of God, and his laws."

Exo 18:17 Moses' father-in-law said to him, "The thing that you do is not good.

Exo 18:18 ***You will surely wear away, both you, and this people that is with you; for the thing is too heavy for you. You are not able to perform it yourself alone.***

Exo 18:19 Listen now to my voice. I will give you counsel, and God be with you. You represent the people before God, and bring the causes to God.

Exo 18:20 You shall teach them the statutes and the laws, and shall show them the way in which they must walk, and the work that they must do.

Exo 18:21 Moreover you shall provide out of all the people able men which fear God: men of truth, hating unjust gain; and place such over them, to be rulers of thousands, rulers of hundreds, rulers of fifties, and rulers of tens.

Exo 18:22 Let them judge the people at all times. It shall be that every great matter they shall bring to you, but every small matter they shall judge themselves. So shall it be easier for you, and they shall share the load with you.

Exo 18:23 If you will do this thing, and God commands you so, then you will be able to endure, and all these people also will go to their place in peace."

TUESDAY Exo 18:24 So Moses listened to the voice of his father-in-law, and did all that he had said.

Exo 18:25 ***Moses chose able men out of all Israel, and made them heads over the people, rulers of thousands, rulers of hundreds, rulers of fifties, and rulers of tens.***

Exo 18:26 They judged the people at all times. They brought the hard causes to Moses, but every small matter they judged themselves.

Exo 18:27 Moses let his father-in-law depart, and he went his way into his own land.

Israel at Mount Sinai

WEDNESDAY Exo 19:1 In the third month after the children of Israel had gone out of the land of Egypt, on that same day they came into the wilderness of Sinai.

Exo 19:2 When they had departed from Rephidim, and had come to the wilderness of Sinai, they encamped in the wilderness; and there Israel encamped before the mountain.

Exo 19:3 Moses went up to God, and YHWH called to him out of the mountain, saying, "This is what you shall tell the house of Jacob, and tell the children of Israel:

Exo 19:4 'You have seen what I did to the Egyptians, and how I bore you on eagles' wings, and brought you to myself.

Exo 19:5 **Now therefore, if you will indeed obey my voice, and keep my covenant, then you shall be my own possession from among all peoples; for all the earth is mine;**

Exo 19:6 and you shall be to me a kingdom of priests, and a holy nation.' These are the words which you shall speak to the children of Israel."

THURSDAY Exo 19:7 Moses came and called for the elders of the people, and set before them all these words which YHWH commanded him.

Exo 19:8 **All the people answered together, and said, "All that YHWH has spoken we will do." Moses reported the words of the people to YHWH.**

Exo 19:9 YHWH said to Moses, "Behold, I come to you in a thick cloud, that the people may hear when I speak with you, and may also believe you forever." Moses told the words of the people to YHWH.

Exo 19:10 YHWH said to Moses, "Go to the people, and sanctify them today and tomorrow, and let them wash their garments,

Exo 19:11 and be ready against the third day; for on the third day YHWH will come down in the sight of all the people on Mount Sinai.

Exo 19:12 You shall set bounds to the people all around, saying, 'Be careful that you don't go up onto the mountain, or touch its border. Whoever touches the mountain shall be surely put to death.

Exo 19:13 No hand shall touch him, but he shall surely be stoned or shot through; whether it is animal or man, he shall not live.' When the trumpet sounds long, they shall come up to the mountain."

Exo 19:14 Moses went down from the mountain to the people, and sanctified the people; and they washed their clothes.

Exo 19:15 He said to the people, "Be ready by the third day. Don't have sexual relations with a woman."

Exo 19:16 On the third day, when it was morning, there were thunders and lightnings, and a thick cloud on the mountain, and the sound of an exceedingly loud trumpet; and all the people who were in the camp trembled.

Exo 19:17 Moses led the people out of the camp to meet God; and they stood at the lower part of the mountain.

page 61

Exo 19:18 All of Mount Sinai smoked, because YHWH descended on it in fire; and its smoke ascended like the smoke of a furnace, and the whole mountain quaked greatly.

Exo 19:19 When the sound of the trumpet grew louder and louder, Moses spoke, and God answered him by a voice.

FRIDAY Exo 19:20 YHWH came down on Mount Sinai, to the top of the mountain. YHWH called Moses to the top of the mountain, and Moses went up.

Exo 19:21 ***YHWH said to Moses, "Go down, warn the people, lest they break through to YHWH to gaze, and many of them perish.***

Exo 19:22 Let the priests also, who come near to YHWH, sanctify themselves, lest YHWH break out on them."

Exo 19:23 Moses said to YHWH, "The people can't come up to Mount Sinai, for you warned us, saying, 'Set bounds around the mountain, and sanctify it.'"

Exo 19:24 YHWH said to him, "Go down! You shall bring Aaron up with you, but don't let the priests and the people break through to come up to YHWH, lest he break out against them."

Exo 19:25 So Moses went down to the people, and told them.

The Ten Commandments

Exo 20:1 God spoke all these words, saying,

Exo 20:2 "I am YHWH your God, who brought you out of the land of Egypt, out of the house of bondage.

Exo 20:3 "You shall have no other gods before me.

Exo 20:4 "You shall not make for yourselves an idol, nor any image of anything that is in the heavens above, or that is in the earth beneath, or that is in the water under the earth:

Exo 20:5 you shall not bow yourself down to them, nor serve them, for I, YHWH your God, am a jealous God, visiting the iniquity of the fathers on the children, on the third and on the fourth generation of those who hate me,

Exo 20:6 and showing loving kindness to thousands of those who love me and keep my commandments.

Exo 20:7 "You shall not take the name of YHWH your God in vain, for YHWH will not hold him guiltless who takes his name in vain.

Exo 20:8 "Remember the Sabbath day, to keep it holy.

Exo 20:9 You shall labor six days, and do all your work,

Exo 20:10 but the seventh day is a Sabbath to YHWH your God. You shall not do any work in it, you, nor your son, nor your daughter, your male servant, nor your female servant, nor your livestock, nor your stranger who is within your gates;

Exo 20:11 for in six days YHWH made heaven and earth, the sea, and all that is in them, and rested the seventh day; therefore YHWH blessed the Sabbath day, and made it holy.

Exo 20:12 "Honor your father and your mother, that your days may be long in the land which YHWH your God gives you.

Exo 20:13 "You shall not murder.

Exo 20:14 "You shall not commit adultery.

Exo 20:15 "You shall not steal.

Exo 20:16 "You shall not give false testimony against your neighbor.

Exo 20:17 "You shall not covet your neighbor's house. You shall not covet your neighbor's wife, nor his male servant, nor his female servant, nor his ox, nor his donkey, nor anything that is your neighbor's."

SABBATH Exo 20:18 All the people perceived the thunderings, the lightnings, the sound of the trumpet, and the mountain smoking. When the people saw it, they trembled, and stayed at a distance.

Exo 20:19 They said to Moses, "Speak with us yourself, and we will listen; but don't let God speak with us, lest we die."

Exo 20:20 **Moses said to the people, "Don't be afraid, for God has come to test you, and that his fear may be before you, that you won't sin."**

Exo 20:21 The people stayed at a distance, and Moses came near to the thick darkness where God was.

Laws About Altars

Exo 20:22 YHWH said to Moses, "This is what you shall tell the children of Israel: 'You yourselves have seen that I have talked with you from heaven.

Exo 20:23 You shall most certainly not make gods of silver or gods of gold for yourselves to be alongside me.

Exo 20:24 You shall make an altar of earth for me, and shall sacrifice on it your burnt offerings and your peace offerings, your sheep and your cattle. In every place where I record my name I will come to you and I will bless you.

Exo 20:25 If you make me an altar of stone, you shall not build it of cut stones; for if you lift up your tool on it, you have polluted it.

Exo 20:26 You shall not go up by steps to my altar, that your nakedness may not be exposed to it.'

CRYPTOGRAM – EXODUS 18:10

A	B	C	D	E	F	G	H	I	J	K	L	M	N	O	P	Q	R	S	T	U	V	W	X	Y	Z
				18					5					11				9							

```
  J  E  _  _  O  S  _  _ , "  _  _  E  S  S  E  _  _  E  _  _  E
  5 18  8 25  4 11  9  2 24 14  23 15 18  9  9 18 14  23 18  8 25 18

  _  O  _  _ , _  O  _  S  _  E  _  E  _  E  _  _  O
 15 11  4 14  20 25 11 25  2  9 14 18 15 24  7 18  4 18 14  3 11 12

  O  _  O  _  _  E  _  _  _  O  _  E  _  _  _  _  _  _  E  _  _  _
 11 12  8 11 13  8 25 18 25  2  6 14 11 13  8 25 18 18 21  3 26  8 24  2  6

  S  _  _  O  _  O  _  _  E  _  _  _  _  _  O  _  _  _  _  _  _  O
  9  2  6 14 11 12  8 11 13  8 25 18 25  2  6 14 11 13 26 25  2  4  2 11

  _  _  _  S  _  E  _  _  _  E  _  _  _  E  _  _  _  _  E  _  O  _  E
 25  2  6 14 25  2  9 14 18 15 24  7 18  4 18 14  8 25 18 26 18 11 26 15 18

  _  O  _  _  E  _  _  _  E  _  _  _  _  O  _  _  E
 13  4 11 10 12  6 14 18  4  8 25 18 25  2  6 14 11 13  8 25 18

  E  _  _  _  _  _  _  S . "
 18 21  3 26  8 24  2  6  9
```

YITRO SCRAMBLE

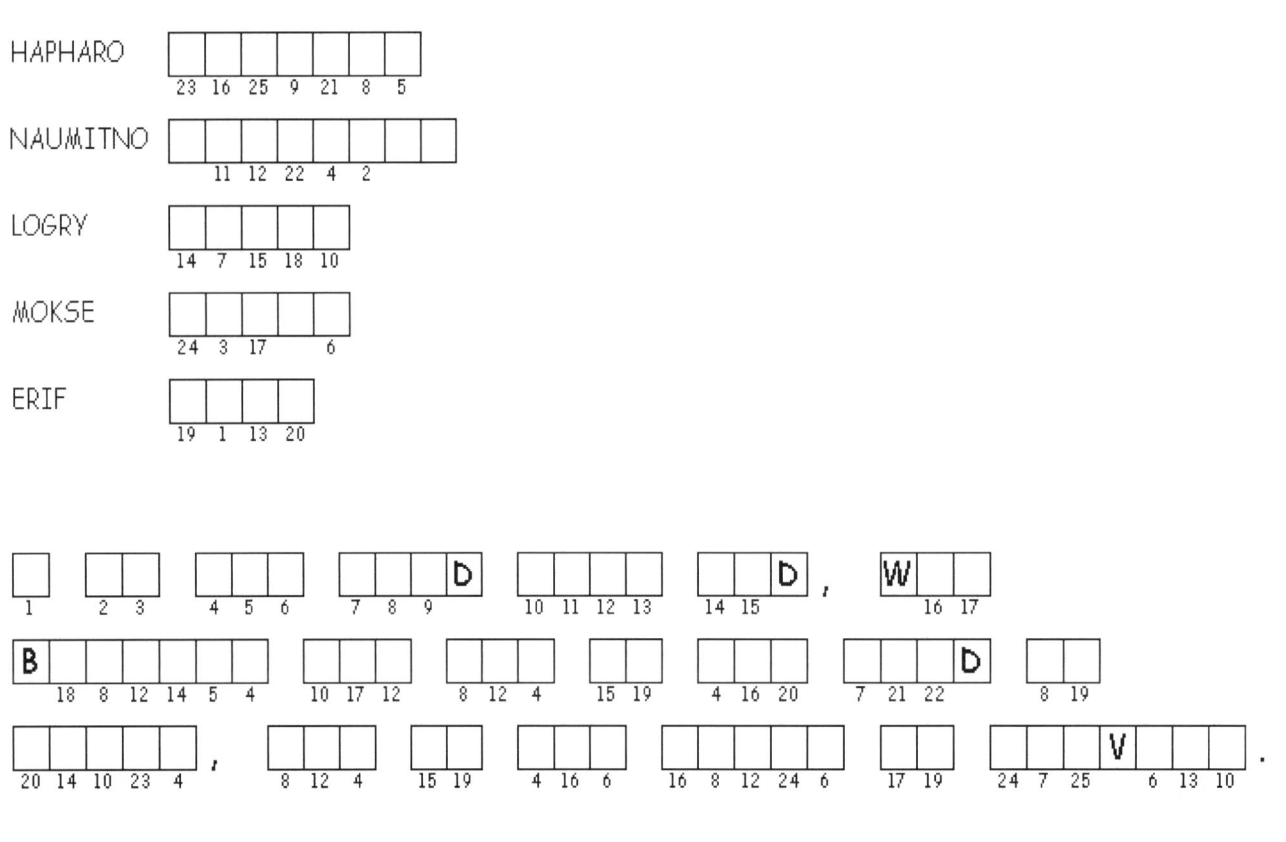

HAPHARO   `23 16 25 9 21 8 5`

NAUMITNO   `11 12 22 4 2`

LOGRY   `14 7 15 18 10`

MOKSE   `24 3 17 6`

ERIF   `19 1 13 20`

page 64

MISHPATIM

מִשְׁפָּטִים

EXODUS

It Means: **Laws**

Our Eighteenth Torah Portion is called Mishpatim! מִשְׁפָּטִים

Exodus 21:1 – Exodus 24:18

PROPHETS: 2 Kings 12:1-16; Isaiah 6:1-5; Jeremiah 33:20-26; 34:8-22; Ezekiel 1:26-28; 8:1,2; Daniel 7:9,10; 10:5,6; Amos 2:9; Zechariah 11:10-14

NEW TESTAMENT: Matthew 5:38-42; 12:1-21; 17:1-11; 26:14-16; Mark 7:6-9; Luke 9:51-56; 10:30-37; Acts 23:1-11; Hebrews 9:15-22, 10:28-39; James 1:27; Revelation 1:13-15; 21:1-14

MAKE A MARK

Each time you hear someone say one of the words below make a "/" beside the word. See how many marks you can get!

| heart |
| plagues |
| blood |
| people |
| hard |
| Israelites |

FIRST FIND

~

If someone mentions a verse or scripture that is NOT in this Torah Portion, see if YOU can be the First to Find it!

Laws About Slaves

SUNDAY Exo 21:1 "Now these are the ordinances which you shall set before them.

Exo 21:2 "*If you buy a Hebrew servant, he shall serve six years and in the seventh he shall go out free without paying anything.*

Exo 21:3 If he comes in by himself, he shall go out by himself. If he is married, then his wife shall go out with him.

Exo 21:4 If his master gives him a wife and she bears him sons or daughters, the wife and her children shall be her master's, and he shall go out by himself.

Exo 21:5 But if the servant shall plainly say, 'I love my master, my wife, and my children. I will not go out free;'

Exo 21:6 then his master shall bring him to God, and shall bring him to the door or to the doorpost, and his master shall bore his ear through with an awl, and he shall serve him forever.

Exo 21:7 "If a man sells his daughter to be a female servant, she shall not go out as the male servants do.

Exo 21:8 If she doesn't please her master, who has married her to himself, then he shall let her be redeemed. He shall have no right to sell her to a foreign people, since he has dealt deceitfully with her.

Exo 21:9 If he marries her to his son, he shall deal with her as a daughter.

Exo 21:10 If he takes another wife to himself, he shall not diminish her food, her clothing, and her marital rights.

Exo 21:11 If he doesn't do these three things for her, she may go free without paying any money.

Exo 21:12 "One who strikes a man so that he dies shall surely be put to death,

Exo 21:13 but not if it is unintentional, but God allows it to happen: then I will appoint you a place where he shall flee.

Exo 21:14 If a man schemes and comes presumptuously on his neighbor to kill him, you shall take him from my altar, that he may die.

Exo 21:15 "Anyone who attacks his father or his mother shall be surely put to death.

Exo 21:16 "Anyone who kidnaps someone and sells him, or if he is found in his hand, he shall surely be put to death.

Exo 21:17 "Anyone who curses his father or his mother shall surely be put to death.

Exo 21:18 "If men quarrel and one strikes the other with a stone, or with his fist, and he doesn't die, but is confined to bed;

Exo 21:19 if he rises again and walks around with his staff, then he who struck him shall be cleared: only he shall pay for the loss of his time, and shall provide for his healing until he is thoroughly healed.

MONDAY Exo 21:20 "If a man strikes his servant or his maid with a rod, and he dies under his hand, he shall surely be punished.

Exo 21:21 Notwithstanding, if he gets up after a day or two, he shall not be punished, for he is his property.

Exo 21:22 "***If men fight and hurt a pregnant woman so that she gives birth prematurely, and yet no harm follows, he shall be surely fined as much as the woman's husband demands and the judges allow.***

Exo 21:23 But if any harm follows, then you must take life for life,

Exo 21:24 eye for eye, tooth for tooth, hand for hand, foot for foot,

Exo 21:25 burning for burning, wound for wound, and bruise for bruise.

Exo 21:26 "If a man strikes his servant's eye, or his maid's eye, and destroys it, he shall let him go free for his eye's sake.

Exo 21:27 If he strikes out his male servant's tooth, or his female servant's tooth, he shall let him go free for his tooth's sake.

Exo 21:28 "If a bull gores a man or a woman to death, the bull shall surely be stoned, and its meat shall not be eaten; but the owner of the bull shall not be held responsible.

Exo 21:29 But if the bull had a habit of goring in the past, and it has been testified to its owner, and he has not kept it in, but it has killed a man or a woman, the bull shall be stoned, and its owner shall also be put to death.

Exo 21:30 If a ransom is laid on him, then he shall give for the redemption of his life whatever is laid on him.

Exo 21:31 Whether it has gored a son or has gored a daughter, according to this judgment it shall be done to him.

Exo 21:32 If the bull gores a male servant or a female servant, thirty shekels of silver shall be given to their master, and the ox shall be stoned.

Laws About Restitution

Exo 21:33 "If a man opens a pit, or if a man digs a pit and doesn't cover it, and a bull or a donkey falls into it,

Exo 21:34 the owner of the pit shall make it good. He shall give money to its owner, and the dead animal shall be his.

Exo 21:35 "If one man's bull injures another's, so that it dies, then they shall sell the live bull, and divide its price; and they shall also divide the dead animal.

Exo 21:36 Or if it is known that the bull was in the habit of goring in the past, and its owner has not kept it in, he shall surely pay bull for bull, and the dead animal shall be his own.

Exo 22:1 "If a man steals an ox or a sheep, and kills it, or sells it; he shall pay five oxen for an ox, and four sheep for a sheep.

Exo 22:2 If the thief is found breaking in, and is struck so that he dies, there shall be no guilt of bloodshed for him.

Exo 22:3 If the sun has risen on him, guilt of bloodshed shall be for him; he shall make restitution. If he has nothing, then he shall be sold for his theft.

TUESDAY Exo 22:4 If the stolen property is found in his hand alive, whether it is ox, donkey, or sheep, he shall pay double.

Exo 22:5 "If a man causes a field or vineyard to be eaten, and lets his animal loose, and it grazes in another man's field, he shall make restitution from the best of his own field, and from the best of his own vineyard.

Exo 22:6 ***"If fire breaks out, and catches in thorns so that the shocks of grain, or the standing grain, or the field are consumed; he who kindled the fire shall surely make restitution.***

Exo 22:7 "If a man delivers to his neighbor money or stuff to keep, and it is stolen out of the man's house; if the thief is found, he shall pay double.

Exo 22:8 If the thief isn't found, then the master of the house shall come near to God, to find out if he hasn't put his hand to his neighbor's goods.

Exo 22:9 For every matter of trespass, whether it is for ox, for donkey, for sheep, for clothing, or for any kind of lost thing, about which one says, 'This is mine,' the cause of both parties shall come before God. He whom God condemns shall pay double to his neighbor.

Exo 22:10 "If a man delivers to his neighbor a donkey, an ox, a sheep, or any animal to keep, and it dies or is injured, or driven away, no man seeing it;

Exo 22:11 the oath of YHWH shall be between them both, whether he hasn't put his hand to his neighbor's goods; and its owner shall accept it, and he shall not make restitution.

Exo 22:12 But if it is stolen from him, he shall make restitution to its owner.

Exo 22:13 If it is torn in pieces, let him bring it for evidence. He shall not make good that which was torn.

Exo 22:14 "If a man borrows anything of his neighbor's, and it is injured, or dies, its owner not being with it, he shall surely make restitution.

Exo 22:15 If its owner is with it, he shall not make it good. If it is a leased thing, it came for its lease.

Laws About Social Justice

Exo 22:16 "If a man entices a virgin who isn't pledged to be married, and lies with her, he shall surely pay a dowry for her to be his wife.

Exo 22:17 If her father utterly refuses to give her to him, he shall pay money according to the dowry of virgins.

Exo 22:18 "You shall not allow a sorceress to live.

Exo 22:19 "Whoever has sex with an animal shall surely be put to death.

Exo 22:20 "He who sacrifices to any god, except to YHWH only, shall be utterly destroyed.

Exo 22:21 "You shall not wrong an alien or oppress him, for you were aliens in the land of Egypt.

Exo 22:22 "You shall not take advantage of any widow or fatherless child.

Exo 22:23 If you take advantage of them at all, and they cry at all to me, I will surely hear their cry;

Exo 22:24 and my wrath will grow hot, and I will kill you with the sword; and your wives shall be widows, and your children fatherless.

Exo 22:25 "If you lend money to any of my people with you who is poor, you shall not be to him as a creditor. You shall not charge him interest.

Exo 22:26 If you take your neighbor's garment as collateral, you shall restore it to him before the sun goes down,

WEDNESDAY Exo 22:27 for that is his only covering, it is his garment for his skin. What would he sleep in? It will happen, when he cries to me, that I will hear, for I am gracious.

Exo 22:28 **"You shall not blaspheme God, nor curse a ruler of your people.**

Exo 22:29 "You shall not delay to offer from your harvest and from the outflow of your presses. "You shall give the firstborn of your sons to me.

Exo 22:30 You shall do likewise with your cattle and with your sheep. Seven days it shall be with its mother, then on the eighth day you shall give it to me.

Exo 22:31 "You shall be holy men to me, therefore you shall not eat any meat that is torn by animals in the field. You shall cast it to the dogs.

Exo 23:1 "You shall not spread a false report. Don't join your hand with the wicked to be a malicious witness.

Exo 23:2 "You shall not follow a crowd to do evil. You shall not testify in court to side with a multitude to pervert justice.

Exo 23:3 You shall not favor a poor man in his cause.

Exo 23:4 "If you meet your enemy's ox or his donkey going astray, you shall surely bring it back to him again.

Exo 23:5 If you see the donkey of him who hates you fallen down under his burden, don't leave him, you shall surely help him with it.

THURSDAY Exo 23:6 "You shall not deny justice to your poor people in their lawsuits.

Exo 23:7 "Keep far from a false charge, and don't kill the innocent and righteous: for I will not justify the wicked.

Exo 23:8 "You shall take no bribe, for a bribe blinds those who have sight and perverts the words of the righteous.

Exo 23:9 "You shall not oppress an alien, for you know the heart of an alien, since you were aliens in the land of Egypt.

Laws About the Sabbath and Festivals

Exo 23:10 "For six years you shall sow your land, and shall gather in its increase,

Exo 23:11 but the seventh year you shall let it rest and lie fallow, that the poor of your people may eat; and what they leave the animal of the field shall eat. In the same way, you shall deal with your vineyard and with your olive grove.

Exo 23:12 "*Six days you shall do your work, and on the seventh day you shall rest, that your ox and your donkey may have rest, and the son of your servant, and the alien may be refreshed.*

Exo 23:13 "Be careful to do all things that I have said to you; and don't invoke the name of other gods or even let them be heard out of your mouth.

Exo 23:14 "You shall observe a feast to me three times a year.

Exo 23:15 You shall observe the feast of unleavened bread. Seven days you shall eat unleavened bread, as I commanded you, at the time appointed in the month Abib (for in it you came out of Egypt), and no one shall appear before me empty.

Exo 23:16 And the feast of harvest, the first fruits of your labors, which you sow in the field; and the feast of ingathering, at the end of the year, when you gather in your labors out of the field.

Exo 23:17 Three times in the year all your males shall appear before the Lord YHWH.

Exo 23:18 "You shall not offer the blood of my sacrifice with leavened bread. The fat of my feast shall not remain all night until the morning.

Exo 23:19 The first of the first fruits of your ground you shall bring into the house of YHWH your God. "You shall not boil a young goat in its mother's milk.

Conquest of Canaan Promised

FRIDAY Exo 23:20 "Behold, I send an angel before you, to keep you by the way, and to bring you into the place which I have prepared.

Exo 23:21 Pay attention to him, and listen to his voice. Don't provoke him, for he will not pardon your disobedience, for my name is in him.

Exo 23:22 But if you indeed listen to his voice, and do all that I speak, then I will be an enemy to your enemies, and an adversary to your adversaries.

Exo 23:23 For my angel shall go before you, and bring you in to the Amorite, the Hittite, the Perizzite, the Canaanite, the Hivite, and the Jebusite; and I will cut them off.

Exo 23:24 **You shall not bow down to their gods, nor serve them, nor follow their practices, but you shall utterly overthrow them and demolish their pillars.**

Exo 23:25 You shall serve YHWH your God, and he will bless your bread and your water, and I will take sickness away from among you.

SABBATH Exo 23:26 No one will miscarry or be barren in your land. I will fulfill the number of your days.

Exo 23:27 I will send my terror before you, and will confuse all the people to whom you come, and I will make all your enemies turn their backs to you.

Exo 23:28 I will send the hornet before you, which will drive out the Hivite, the Canaanite, and the Hittite, from before you.

Exo 23:29 I will not drive them out from before you in one year, lest the land become desolate, and the animals of the field multiply against you.

Exo 23:30 **Little by little I will drive them out from before you, until you have increased and inherit the land.**

Exo 23:31 I will set your border from the Red Sea even to the sea of the Philistines, and from the wilderness to the River; for I will deliver the inhabitants of the land into your hand, and you shall drive them out before you.

Exo 23:32 You shall make no covenant with them, nor with their gods.

Exo 23:33 They shall not dwell in your land, lest they make you sin against me, for if you serve their gods, it will surely be a snare to you."

The Covenant Confirmed

Exo 24:1 He said to Moses, "Come up to YHWH, you, and Aaron, Nadab, and Abihu, and seventy of the elders of Israel; and worship from a distance.

Exo 24:2 Moses alone shall come near to YHWH, but they shall not come near. The people shall not go up with him."

Exo 24:3 Moses came and told the people all YHWH's words, and all the ordinances; and all the people answered with one voice, and said, "All the words which YHWH has spoken will we do."

Exo 24:4 Moses wrote all YHWH's words, and rose up early in the morning, and built an altar under the mountain, and twelve pillars for the twelve tribes of Israel.

Exo 24:5 He sent young men of the children of Israel, who offered burnt offerings and sacrificed peace offerings of cattle to YHWH.

Exo 24:6 Moses took half of the blood and put it in basins, and half of the blood he sprinkled on the altar.

Exo 24:7 He took the book of the covenant and read it in the hearing of the people, and they said, "All that YHWH has spoken will we do, and be obedient."

Exo 24:8 Moses took the blood, and sprinkled it on the people, and said, "Look, this is the blood of the covenant, which YHWH has made with you concerning all these words."

Exo 24:9 Then Moses, Aaron, Nadab, Abihu, and seventy of the elders of Israel went up.

Exo 24:10 They saw the God of Israel. Under his feet was like a paved work of sapphire stone, like the skies for clearness.

Exo 24:11 He didn't lay his hand on the nobles of the children of Israel. They saw God, and ate and drank.

Exo 24:12 YHWH said to Moses, "Come up to me on the mountain, and stay here, and I will give you the stone tablets with the law and the commands that I have written, that you may teach them."

Exo 24:13 Moses rose up with Joshua, his servant, and Moses went up onto God's Mountain.

Exo 24:14 He said to the elders, "Wait here for us, until we come again to you. Behold, Aaron and Hur are with you. Whoever is involved in a dispute can go to them."

Exo 24:15 Moses went up on the mountain, and the cloud covered the mountain.

Exo 24:16 YHWH's glory settled on Mount Sinai, and the cloud covered it six days. The seventh day he called to Moses out of the middle of the cloud.

Exo 24:17 The appearance of YHWH's glory was like devouring fire on the top of the mountain in the eyes of the children of Israel.

Exo 24:18 Moses entered into the middle of the cloud, and went up on the mountain; and Moses was on the mountain forty days and forty nights.

MY NOTES

CRYPTOGRAM-Daniel 7:9-10

A	B	C	D	E	F	G	H	I	J	K	L	M	N	O	P	Q	R	S	T	U	V	W	X	Y	Z
14		26						11						12			19		5			25			

page 75

MISHPATIM WORDFIND

```
S S N Y I A C T H D P S A P T
Y T Z I A F R L E K L E A A U
W K N R A U R N O O Q L B S O
V Z O E M T E Z O U I C D S V
F N J P M V N F J O D A M O A
F E E C A D V U J D F N O V H
N T I E P G N Y O H E R S E S
S F L T E E A A P M M E E R W
T N H W K H N K M G B B S X E
U S U K K O T T P M N A O G S
I S R A E L I T E S O T K T F
B E P A X G V B R C M C S T Y
R V X C R U L K A C O A T D A
T N A N E V O C T I E S C J H
B Y D K Q V V M H F L O T V S
```

AARON
COVENANT
MOSES
PENTECOST
TABERNACLES

CLOUD
FEASTS
MOUNTAIN
SHAVOUT
TRUMPETS

COMMANDMENTS
ISRAELITES
PASSOVER
SUKKOT
UNLEAVENED

VERSE FIND – EXODUS 22:28

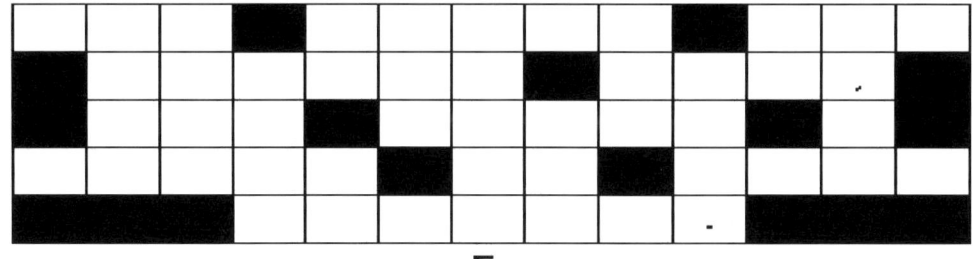

```
                    E
    N U E R C U R L
    U L V E O P L S Y N U
  Y R O P I L A F G O D O T
  R O E R S H O L E E O A R
```

page 76

TERUMAH

תְּרוּמָה

EXODUS

It Means: **Offering**

Our Ninteenth Torah Portion is called Terumah! תְּרוּמָה
Exodus 25:1 – Exodus 27:19
PROPHETS: 1 Kings 5:1-6:13
NEW TESTAMENT: Matthew 5:33-37; Hebrews 8:1-6, 9:23-24, 10:1

MAKE A MARK

Each time you hear someone say one of the words below make a '**/**" beside the word. See how many marks you can get!

heart	
plagues	
blood	
people	
hard	
Israelites	

FIRST FIND

~

If someone mentions a verse or scripture that is NOT in this Torah Portion, see if YOU can be the First to Find it!

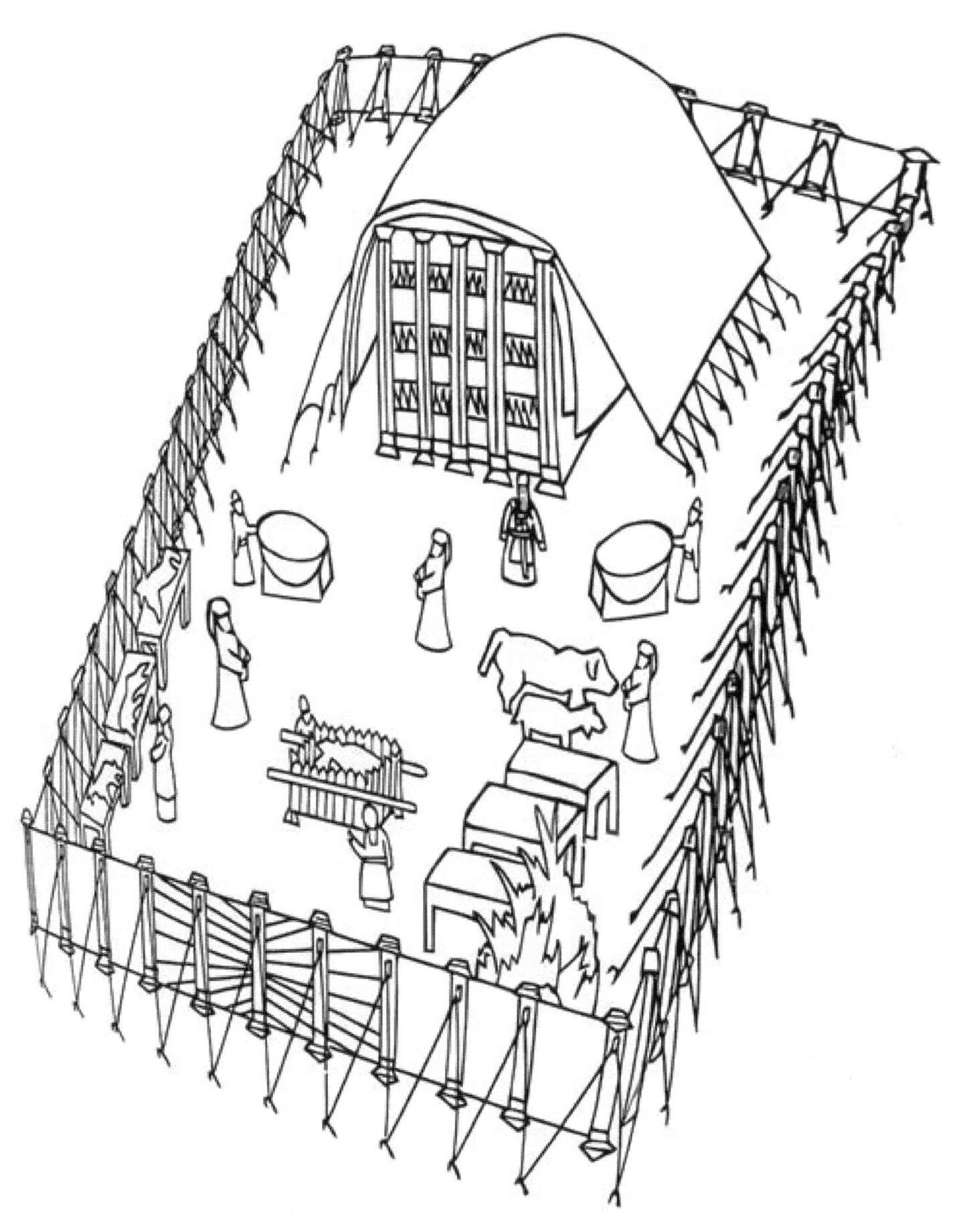

Contributions for the Sanctuary

<u>SUNDAY</u> Exo 25:1 YHWH spoke to Moses, saying,

Exo 25:2 "Speak to the children of Israel, that they take an offering for me. From everyone whose heart makes him willing you shall take my offering.

Exo 25:3 This is the offering which you shall take from them: gold, silver, brass,

Exo 25:4 blue, purple, scarlet, fine linen, goats' hair,

Exo 25:5 rams' skins dyed red, sea cow hides, acacia wood,

Exo 25:6 oil for the light, spices for the anointing oil and for the sweet incense,

Exo 25:7 onyx stones, and stones to be set for the ephod and for the breastplate.

Exo 25:8 Let them make me a sanctuary, that I may dwell among them.

Exo 25:9 According to all that I show you, the pattern of the tabernacle, and the pattern of all of its furniture, even so you shall make it.

The Ark of the Covenant

Exo 25:10 "They shall make an ark of acacia wood. Its length shall be two and a half cubits, its width a cubit and a half, and a cubit and a half its height.

Exo 25:11 You shall overlay it with pure gold. You shall overlay it inside and outside, and you shall make a gold molding around it.

Exo 25:12 You shall cast four rings of gold for it, and put them in its four feet. Two rings shall be on the one side of it, and two rings on the other side of it.

Exo 25:13 You shall make poles of acacia wood, and overlay them with gold.

Exo 25:14 You shall put the poles into the rings on the sides of the ark to carry the ark.

Exo 25:15 The poles shall be in the rings of the ark. They shall not be taken from it.

Exo 25:16 **You shall put the testimony which I shall give you into the ark.**

<u>MONDAY</u> Exo 25:17 You shall make a mercy seat of pure gold. Two and a half cubits shall be its length, and a cubit and a half its width.

Exo 25:18 You shall make two cherubim of hammered gold. You shall make them at the two ends of the mercy seat.

Exo 25:19 Make one cherub at the one end, and one cherub at the other end. You shall make the cherubim on its two ends of one piece with the mercy seat.

Exo 25:20 The cherubim shall spread out their wings upward, covering the mercy seat with their wings, with their faces toward one another. The faces of the cherubim shall be toward the mercy seat.

Exo 25:21 You shall put the mercy seat on top of the ark, and in the ark you shall put the testimony that I will give you.

Exo 25:22 ***There I will meet with you, and I will tell you from above the mercy seat, from between the two cherubim which are on the ark of the testimony, all that I command you for the children of Israel.***

The Table for Bread

Exo 25:23 "You shall make a table of acacia wood. Two cubits shall be its length, and a cubit its width, and one and a half cubits its height.

Exo 25:24 You shall overlay it with pure gold, and make a gold molding around it.

Exo 25:25 You shall make a rim of a hand width around it. You shall make a golden molding on its rim around it.

Exo 25:26 You shall make four rings of gold for it, and put the rings in the four corners that are on its four feet.

Exo 25:27 the rings shall be close to the rim, for places for the poles to carry the table.

Exo 25:28 You shall make the poles of acacia wood, and overlay them with gold, that the table may be carried with them.

Exo 25:29 You shall make its dishes, its spoons, its ladles, and its bowls to pour out offerings with. You shall make them of pure gold.

Exo 25:30 You shall set bread of the presence on the table before me always.

The Golden Lampstand

TUESDAY Exo 25:31 "You shall make a lamp stand of pure gold. Of hammered work shall the lamp stand be made, even its base, its shaft, its cups, its buds, and its flowers, shall be of one piece with it.

Exo 25:32 There shall be six branches going out of its sides: three branches of the lamp stand out of its one side, and three branches of the lamp stand out of its other side;

Exo 25:33 three cups made like almond blossoms in one branch, a bud and a flower; and three cups made like almond blossoms in the other branch, a bud and a flower, so for the six branches going out of the lamp stand;

Exo 25:34 and in the lamp stand four cups made like almond blossoms, its buds and its flowers;

Exo 25:35 and a bud under two branches of one piece with it, and a bud under two branches of one piece with it, and a bud under two branches of one piece with it, for the six branches going out of the lamp stand.

Exo 25:36 Their buds and their branches shall be of one piece with it, all of it one beaten work of pure gold.

Exo 25:37 You shall make its lamps seven, and they shall light its lamps to give light to the space in front of it.

Exo 25:38 Its snuffers and its snuff dishes shall be of pure gold.

Exo 25:39 It shall be made of a talent of pure gold, with all these accessories.

Exo 25:40 **See that you make them after their pattern, which has been shown to you on the mountain.**

The Tabernacle

Exo 26:1 "Moreover you shall make the tabernacle with ten curtains; of fine twined linen, and blue, and purple, and scarlet, with cherubim. The work of the skillful workman you shall make them.

Exo 26:2 The length of each curtain shall be twenty-eight cubits, and the width of each curtain four cubits: all the curtains shall have one measure.

Exo 26:3 Five curtains shall be coupled together to one another; and the other five curtains shall be coupled to one another.

Exo 26:4 You shall make loops of blue on the edge of the one curtain from the edge in the coupling; and likewise you shall make in the edge of the curtain that is outermost in the second coupling.

Exo 26:5 You shall make fifty loops in the one curtain, and you shall make fifty loops in the edge of the curtain that is in the second coupling. The loops shall be opposite one another.

Exo 26:6 You shall make fifty clasps of gold, and couple the curtains to one another with the clasps: and the tabernacle shall be a unit.

Exo 26:7 "You shall make curtains of goats' hair for a covering over the tabernacle. You shall make them eleven curtains.

Exo 26:8 The length of each curtain shall be thirty cubits, and the width of each curtain four cubits: the eleven curtains shall have one measure.

Exo 26:9 You shall couple five curtains by themselves, and six curtains by themselves, and shall double over the sixth curtain in the forefront of the tent.

Exo 26:10 You shall make fifty loops on the edge of the one curtain that is outermost in the coupling, and fifty loops on the edge of the curtain which is outermost in the second coupling.

Exo 26:11 You shall make fifty clasps of brass, and put the clasps into the loops, and couple the tent together, that it may be one.

Exo 26:12 The overhanging part that remains of the curtains of the tent, the half curtain that remains, shall hang over the back of the tabernacle.

Exo 26:13 The cubit on the one side, and the cubit on the other side, of that which remains in the length of the curtains of the tent, shall hang over the sides of the tabernacle on this side and on that side, to cover it.

Exo 26:14 You shall make a covering for the tent of rams' skins dyed red, and a covering of sea cow hides above.

WEDNESDAY Exo 26:15 "You shall make the boards for the tabernacle of acacia wood, standing up.

Exo 26:16 Ten cubits shall be the length of a board, and one and a half cubits the width of each board.

Exo 26:17 There shall be two tenons in each board, joined to one another: thus you shall make for all the boards of the tabernacle.

Exo 26:18 You shall make the boards for the tabernacle, twenty boards for the south side southward.

Exo 26:19 You shall make forty sockets of silver under the twenty boards; two sockets under one board for its two tenons, and two sockets under another board for its two tenons.

Exo 26:20 For the second side of the tabernacle, on the north side, twenty boards,

Exo 26:21 and their forty sockets of silver; two sockets under one board, and two sockets under another board.

Exo 26:22 For the far part of the tabernacle westward you shall make six boards.

Exo 26:23 You shall make two boards for the corners of the tabernacle in the far part.

Exo 26:24 They shall be double beneath, and in the same way they shall be whole to its top to one ring: thus shall it be for them both; they shall be for the two corners.

Exo 26:25 There shall be eight boards, and their sockets of silver, sixteen sockets; two sockets under one board, and two sockets under another board.

Exo 26:26 "You shall make bars of acacia wood: five for the boards of the one side of the tabernacle,

Exo 26:27 and five bars for the boards of the other side of the tabernacle, and five bars for the boards of the side of the tabernacle, for the far part westward.

Exo 26:28 The middle bar in the middle of the boards shall pass through from end to end.

Exo 26:29 You shall overlay the boards with gold, and make their rings of gold for places for the bars: and you shall overlay the bars with gold.

Exo 26:30 **You shall set up the tabernacle according to the way that it was shown to you on the mountain.**

THURSDAY Exo 26:31 "You shall make a veil of blue, and purple, and scarlet, and fine twined linen, with cherubim. The work of the skillful workman shall it be made.

Exo 26:32 You shall hang it on four pillars of acacia overlaid with gold; their hooks shall be of gold, on four sockets of silver.

Exo 26:33 You shall hang up the veil under the clasps, and shall bring the ark of the testimony in there within the veil: and the veil shall separate the holy place from the most holy for you.

Exo 26:34 **You shall put the mercy seat on the ark of the testimony in the most holy place.**

Exo 26:35 You shall set the table outside the veil, and the lamp stand over against the table on the side of the tabernacle toward the south: and you shall put the table on the north side.

Exo 26:36 "You shall make a screen for the door of the Tent, of blue, and purple, and scarlet, and fine twined linen, the work of the embroiderer.

Exo 26:37 You shall make for the screen five pillars of acacia, and overlay them with gold: their hooks shall be of gold: and you shall cast five sockets of brass for them.

The Bronze Altar

FRIDAY Exo 27:1 "You shall make the altar of acacia wood, five cubits long, and five cubits wide; the altar shall be square: and its height shall be three cubits.

Exo 27:2 You shall make its horns on its four corners; its horns shall be of one piece with it; and you shall overlay it with brass.

Exo 27:3 You shall make its pots to take away its ashes, its shovels, its basins, its meat hooks, and its fire pans: all its vessels you shall make of brass.

Exo 27:4 You shall make a grating for it of network of brass: and on the net you shall make four bronze rings in its four corners.

Exo 27:5 You shall put it under the ledge around the altar beneath, that the net may reach halfway up the altar.

Exo 27:6 You shall make poles for the altar, poles of acacia wood, and overlay them with brass.

Exo 27:7 Its poles shall be put into the rings, and the poles shall be on the two sides of the altar, when carrying it.

Exo 27:8 **You shall make it with hollow planks. They shall make it as it has been shown you on the mountain.**

The Court of the Tabernacle

SABBATH Exo 27:9 *"You shall make the court of the tabernacle: for the south side southward there shall be hangings for the court of fine twined linen one hundred cubits long for one side:*

Exo 27:10 and its pillars shall be twenty, and their sockets twenty, of brass; the hooks of the pillars and their fillets shall be of silver.

Exo 27:11 Likewise for the north side in length there shall be hangings one hundred cubits long, and its pillars twenty, and their sockets twenty, of brass; the hooks of the pillars, and their fillets, of silver.

Exo 27:12 For the width of the court on the west side shall be hangings of fifty cubits; their pillars ten, and their sockets ten.

Exo 27:13 The width of the court on the east side eastward shall be fifty cubits.

Exo 27:14 The hangings for the one side of the gate shall be fifteen cubits; their pillars three, and their sockets three.

Exo 27:15 For the other side shall be hangings of fifteen cubits; their pillars three, and their sockets three.

Exo 27:16 For the gate of the court shall be a screen of twenty cubits, of blue, and purple, and scarlet, and fine twined linen, the work of the embroiderer; their pillars four, and their sockets four.

Exo 27:17 All the pillars of the court around shall be filleted with silver; their hooks of silver, and their sockets of brass.

Exo 27:18 The length of the court shall be one hundred cubits, and the width fifty throughout, and the height five cubits, of fine twined linen, and their sockets of brass.

Exo 27:19 All the instruments of the tabernacle in all its service, and all its pins, and all the pins of the court, shall be of brass.

MY NOTES

EXODUS 25:10-21 "They shall make an ark of acacia wood. Two cubits and a half shall be its length, a cubit and a half its breadth, and a cubit and a half its height. You shall overlay it with pure gold, inside and outside shall you overlay it, and you shall make on it a molding of gold around it. You shall cast four rings of gold for it and put them on its four feet, two rings on the one side of it, and two rings on the other side of it. You shall make poles of acacia wood and overlay them with gold. And you shall put the poles into the rings on the sides of the ark to carry the ark by them. The poles shall remain in the rings of the ark; they shall not be taken from it. And you shall put into the ark the testimony that I shall give you."

"You shall make a mercy seat of pure gold. Two cubits and a half shall be its length, and a cubit and a half its breadth. And you shall make two cherubim of gold; of hammered work shall you make them, on the two ends of the mercy seat. Make one cherub on the one end, and one cherub on the other end. Of one piece with the mercy seat shall you make the cherubim on its two ends. The cherubim shall spread out their wings above, overshadowing the mercy seat with their wings, their faces one to another; toward the mercy seat shall the faces of the cherubim be. And you shall put the mercy seat on the top of the ark, and in the ark you shall put the testimony that I shall give you."

TERUMAH WORDFIND

Across
1. a place inside the tabernacle
5. a place where people gather
6. a large place of worship
7. fuel for the lamps

Down
2. the type of wood the ark was made of
3. a place where sacrifices are performed
4. a seven branched lamp stand
5. a type of angelic being

VERSE FIND – EXODUS 25:2

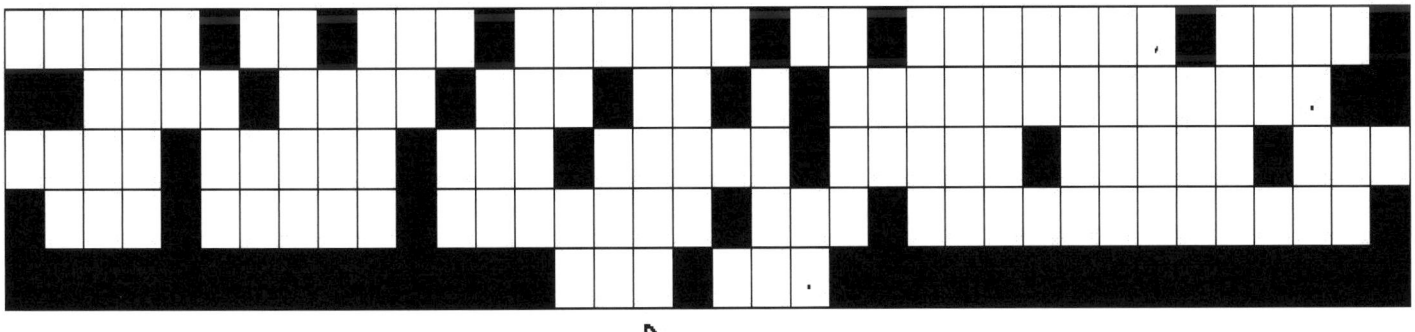

page 87

TETZAVEH

EXODUS

It Means: **You Shall Command**

Our Twentieth Torah Portion is called Tetzaveh! תְּצַוֶּה
Exodus 27:20 – Exodus 30:10

PROPHETS: 1 Samuel 15:2-34; Isaiah 9:6,7; 60:19,20; Ezekiel 28:11-19; 43:10-27; 44:9-18
NEW TESTAMENT: Romans 12:1-13:14; Philippians 4:4-20; Revelation 21:16-27

MAKE A MARK

Each time you hear someone say one of the words below make a '/" beside the word. See how many marks you can get!

heart	
plagues	
blood	
people	
hard	
Israelites	

FIRST FIND

~

If someone mentions a verse or scripture that is NOT in this Torah Portion, see if YOU can be the First to Find it!

THE HIGH PRIESTS' GARMENTS

Exodus 28

Moses' brother, Aaron was to serve as High Priest in the Tabernacle.
God had talented craftsmen to make special clothing for Aaron.
How many articles of clothing can you name?

1. _____
2. _____
3. _____
4. _____
5. _____
6. _____
7. _____
8. _____
9. _____
10. _____

BONUS: FILL IN THE BLANKS

EXODUS 29:46 And they shall know that I am the _____ _____ _____, who brought them out of the land of _____ that I might _____ among them. I am the Lord their God.

page 90

Oil for the Lamp

<u>SUNDAY</u> Exo 27:20 "You shall command the children of Israel, that they bring to you pure olive oil beaten for the light, to cause a lamp to burn continually.

Exo 27:21 In the Tent of Meeting, outside the veil which is before the testimony, Aaron and his sons shall keep it in order from evening to morning before YHWH: it shall be a statute forever throughout their generations on the behalf of the children of Israel.

The Priests' Garments

Exo 28:1 "Bring Aaron your brother, and his sons with him, near to you from among the children of Israel, that he may minister to me in the priest's office, even Aaron, Nadab and Abihu, Eleazar and Ithamar, Aaron's sons.

Exo 28:2 You shall make holy garments for Aaron your brother, for glory and for beauty.

Exo 28:3 **You shall speak to all who are wise-hearted, whom I have filled with the spirit of wisdom, that they make Aaron's garments to sanctify him, that he may minister to me in the priest's office.**

Exo 28:4 These are the garments which they shall make: a breastplate, and an ephod, and a robe, and a coat of checker work, a turban, and a sash: and they shall make holy garments for Aaron your brother, and his sons, that he may minister to me in the priest's office.

Exo 28:5 They shall take the gold, and the blue, and the purple, and the scarlet, and the fine linen.

Exo 28:6 "They shall make the ephod of gold, of blue, and purple, scarlet, and fine twined linen, the work of the skillful workman.

Exo 28:7 It shall have two shoulder straps joined to the two ends of it, that it may be joined together.

Exo 28:8 The skillfully woven band, which is on it, that is on him, shall be like its work and of the same piece; of gold, of blue, and purple, and scarlet, and fine twined linen.

Exo 28:9 You shall take two onyx stones, and engrave on them the names of the children of Israel:

Exo 28:10 six of their names on the one stone, and the names of the six that remain on the other stone, in the order of their birth.

Exo 28:11 With the work of an engraver in stone, like the engravings of a signet, you shall engrave the two stones, according to the names of the children of Israel: you shall make them to be enclosed in settings of gold.

Exo 28:12 You shall put the two stones on the shoulder straps of the ephod, to be stones of memorial for the children of Israel: and Aaron shall bear their names before YHWH on his two shoulders for a memorial.

MONDAY Exo 28:13 You shall make settings of gold,

Exo 28:14 and two chains of pure gold; you shall make them like cords of braided work: and you shall put the braided chains on the settings.

Exo 28:15 "You shall make a breastplate of judgment, the work of the skillful workman; like the work of the ephod you shall make it; of gold, of blue, and purple, and scarlet, and fine twined linen, you shall make it.

Exo 28:16 It shall be square and folded double; a span shall be its length of it, and a span its width.

Exo 28:17 You shall set in it settings of stones, four rows of stones: a row of ruby, topaz, and beryl shall be the first row;

Exo 28:18 and the second row a turquoise, a sapphire, and an emerald;

Exo 28:19 and the third row a jacinth, an agate, and an amethyst;

Exo 28:20 and the fourth row a chrysolite, an onyx, and a jasper: they shall be enclosed in gold in their settings.

Exo 28:21 **The stones shall be according to the names of the children of Israel, twelve, according to their names; like the engravings of a signet, everyone according to his name, they shall be for the twelve tribes.**

Exo 28:22 You shall make on the breastplate chains like cords, of braided work of pure gold.

Exo 28:23 You shall make on the breastplate two rings of gold, and shall put the two rings on the two ends of the breastplate.

Exo 28:24 You shall put the two braided chains of gold in the two rings at the ends of the breastplate.

Exo 28:25 The other two ends of the two braided chains you shall put on the two settings, and put them on the shoulder straps of the ephod in its forepart.

Exo 28:26 You shall make two rings of gold, and you shall put them on the two ends of the breastplate, on its edge, which is toward the side of the ephod inward.

Exo 28:27 You shall make two rings of gold, and shall put them on the two shoulder straps of the ephod underneath, in its forepart, close by its coupling, above the skillfully woven band of the ephod.

Exo 28:28 They shall bind the breastplate by its rings to the rings of the ephod with a lace of blue, that it may be on the skillfully woven band of the ephod, and that the breastplate may not swing out from the ephod.

Exo 28:29 Aaron shall bear the names of the children of Israel in the breastplate of judgment on his heart, when he goes in to the holy place, for a memorial before YHWH continually.

Exo 28:30 You shall put in the breastplate of judgment the Urim and the Thummim; and they shall be on Aaron's heart, when he goes in before YHWH: and Aaron shall bear the judgment of the children of Israel on his heart before YHWH continually.

TUESDAY Exo 28:31 "You shall make the robe of the ephod all of blue.

Exo 28:32 It shall have a hole for the head in the middle of it. It shall have a binding of woven work around its hole, as it were the hole of a coat of mail, that it not be torn.

Exo 28:33 On its hem you shall make pomegranates of blue, and of purple, and of scarlet, around its hem; and bells of gold between and around them:

Exo 28:34 a golden bell and a pomegranate, a golden bell and a pomegranate, around the hem of the robe.

Exo 28:35 It shall be on Aaron to minister: and its sound shall be heard when he goes in to the holy place before YHWH, and when he comes out, that he not die.

Exo 28:36 ***"You shall make a plate of pure gold, and engrave on it, like the engravings of a signet, 'HOLY TO YHWH.'***

Exo 28:37 You shall put it on a lace of blue, and it shall be on the sash; on the front of the sash it shall be.

Exo 28:38 It shall be on Aaron's forehead, and Aaron shall bear the iniquity of the holy things, which the children of Israel shall make holy in all their holy gifts; and it shall be always on his forehead, that they may be accepted before YHWH.

Exo 28:39 You shall weave the coat in checker work of fine linen, and you shall make a turban of fine linen, and you shall make a sash, the work of the embroiderer.

Exo 28:40 "You shall make coats for Aaron's sons, and you shall make sashes for them and you shall make headbands for them, for glory and for beauty.

Exo 28:41 You shall put them on Aaron your brother, and on his sons with him, and shall anoint them, and consecrate them, and sanctify them, that they may minister to me in the priest's office.

Exo 28:42 You shall make them linen breeches to cover the flesh of their nakedness; from the waist even to the thighs they shall reach:

Exo 28:43 They shall be on Aaron, and on his sons, when they go in to the Tent of Meeting, or when they come near to the altar to minister in the holy place; that they don't bear iniquity, and die: it shall be a statute forever to him and to his offspring after him.

Consecration of the Priests

WEDNESDAY Exo 29:1 "This is the thing that you shall do to them to make them holy, to minister to me in the priest's office: take one young bull and two rams without defect,

Exo 29:2 unleavened bread, unleavened cakes mixed with oil, and unleavened wafers anointed with oil: you shall make them of fine wheat flour.

Exo 29:3 You shall put them into one basket, and bring them in the basket, with the bull and the two rams.

Exo 29:4 You shall bring Aaron and his sons to the door of the Tent of Meeting, and shall wash them with water.

Exo 29:5 You shall take the garments, and put on Aaron the coat, the robe of the ephod, the ephod, and the breastplate, and clothe him with the skillfully woven band of the ephod;

Exo 29:6 and you shall set the turban on his head, and put the holy crown on the turban.

Exo 29:7 **Then you shall take the anointing oil, and pour it on his head, and anoint him.**

Exo 29:8 You shall bring his sons, and put coats on them.

Exo 29:9 You shall clothe them with belts, Aaron and his sons, and bind headbands on them: and they shall have the priesthood by a perpetual statute: and you shall consecrate Aaron and his sons.

Exo 29:10 "You shall bring the bull before the Tent of Meeting: and Aaron and his sons shall lay their hands on the head of the bull.

Exo 29:11 You shall kill the bull before YHWH, at the door of the Tent of Meeting.

Exo 29:12 You shall take of the blood of the bull, and put it on the horns of the altar with your finger; and you shall pour out all the blood at the base of the altar.

Exo 29:13 You shall take all the fat that covers the innards, the cover of the liver, the two kidneys, and the fat that is on them, and burn them on the altar.

Exo 29:14 But the meat of the bull, and its skin, and its dung, you shall burn with fire outside of the camp: it is a sin offering.

Exo 29:15 "You shall also take the one ram; and Aaron and his sons shall lay their hands on the head of the ram.

Exo 29:16 You shall kill the ram, and you shall take its blood, and sprinkle it around on the altar.

Exo 29:17 You shall cut the ram into its pieces, and wash its innards, and its legs, and put them with its pieces, and with its head.

Exo 29:18 You shall burn the whole ram on the altar: it is a burnt offering to YHWH; it is a pleasant aroma, an offering made by fire to YHWH.

THURSDAY Exo 29:19 "You shall take the other ram; and Aaron and his sons shall lay their hands on the head of the ram.

Exo 29:20 Then you shall kill the ram, and take some of its blood, and put it on the tip of the right ear of Aaron, and on the tip of the right ear of his sons, and on the thumb of their right hand, and on the big toe of their right foot, and sprinkle the blood around on the altar.

Exo 29:21 You shall take of the blood that is on the altar, and of the anointing oil, and sprinkle it on Aaron, and on his garments, and on his sons, and on the garments of his sons with him: and he shall be made holy, and his garments, and his sons, and his sons' garments with him.

Exo 29:22 Also you shall take some of the ram's fat, the fat tail, the fat that covers the innards, the cover of the liver, the two kidneys, the fat that is on them, and the right thigh (for it is a ram of consecration),

Exo 29:23 and one loaf of bread, one cake of oiled bread, and one wafer out of the basket of unleavened bread that is before YHWH.

Exo 29:24 ***You shall put all of this in Aaron's hands, and in his sons' hands, and shall wave them for a wave offering before YHWH.***

Exo 29:25 You shall take them from their hands, and burn them on the altar on the burnt offering, for a pleasant aroma before YHWH: it is an offering made by fire to YHWH.

Exo 29:26 "You shall take the breast of Aaron's ram of consecration, and wave it for a wave offering before YHWH: and it shall be your portion.

Exo 29:27 You shall sanctify the breast of the wave offering, and the thigh of the wave offering, which is waved, and which is heaved up, of the ram of consecration, even of that which is for Aaron, and of that which is for his sons:

Exo 29:28 and it shall be for Aaron and his sons as their portion forever from the children of Israel; for it is a wave offering: and it shall be a wave offering from the children of Israel of the sacrifices of their peace offerings, even their wave offering to YHWH.

Exo 29:29 "The holy garments of Aaron shall be for his sons after him, to be anointed in them, and to be consecrated in them.

Exo 29:30 Seven days shall the son who is priest in his place put them on, when he comes into the Tent of Meeting to minister in the holy place.

MY NOTES

Exo 29:31 "You shall take the ram of consecration, and boil its meat in a holy place.

Exo 29:32 Aaron and his sons shall eat the meat of the ram, and the bread that is in the basket, at the door of the Tent of Meeting.

Exo 29:33 They shall eat those things with which atonement was made, to consecrate and sanctify them: but a stranger shall not eat of it, because they are holy.

Exo 29:34 If anything of the meat of the consecration, or of the bread, remains to the morning, then you shall burn the remainder with fire: it shall not be eaten, because it is holy.

Exo 29:35 "You shall do so to Aaron, and to his sons, according to all that I have commanded you. You shall consecrate them seven days.

Exo 29:36 Every day you shall offer the bull of sin offering for atonement: and you shall cleanse the altar, when you make atonement for it; and you shall anoint it, to sanctify it.

Exo 29:37 Seven days you shall make atonement for the altar, and sanctify it: and the altar shall be most holy; whatever touches the altar shall be holy.

FRIDAY Exo 29:38 "Now this is that which you shall offer on the altar: two lambs a year old day by day continually.

Exo 29:39 The one lamb you shall offer in the morning; and the other lamb you shall offer at evening:

Exo 29:40 and with the one lamb a tenth part of an ephah of fine flour mixed with the fourth part of a hin of beaten oil, and the fourth part of a hin of wine for a drink offering.

Exo 29:41 The other lamb you shall offer at evening, and shall do to it according to the meal offering of the morning, and according to its drink offering, for a pleasant aroma, an offering made by fire to YHWH.

Exo 29:42 It shall be a continual burnt offering throughout your generations at the door of the Tent of Meeting before YHWH, where I will meet with you, to speak there to you.

Exo 29:43 There I will meet with the children of Israel; and the place shall be sanctified by my glory.

Exo 29:44 I will sanctify the Tent of Meeting and the altar: Aaron also and his sons I will sanctify, to minister to me in the priest's office.

Exo 29:45 I will dwell among the children of Israel, and will be their God.

Exo 29:46 They shall know that I am YHWH their God, who brought them out of the land of Egypt, that I might dwell among them: I am YHWH their God.

The Altar of Incense

SABBATH Exo 30:1 "You shall make an altar to burn incense on. You shall make it of acacia wood.

Exo 30:2 Its length shall be a cubit, and its width a cubit. It shall be square, and its height shall be two cubits. Its horns shall be of one piece with it.

Exo 30:3 You shall overlay it with pure gold, its top, its sides around it, and its horns; and you shall make a gold molding around it.

Exo 30:4 You shall make two golden rings for it under its molding; on its two ribs, on its two sides you shall make them; and they shall be for places for poles with which to bear it.

Exo 30:5 You shall make the poles of acacia wood, and overlay them with gold.

Exo 30:6 You shall put it before the veil that is by the ark of the testimony, before the mercy seat that is over the testimony, where I will meet with you.

Exo 30:7 Aaron shall burn incense of sweet spices on it every morning. When he tends the lamps, he shall burn it.

Exo 30:8 When Aaron lights the lamps at evening, he shall burn it, a perpetual incense before YHWH throughout your generations.

Exo 30:9 ***You shall offer no strange incense on it, nor burnt offering, nor meal offering; and you shall pour no drink offering on it.***

Exo 30:10 Aaron shall make atonement on its horns once in the year; with the blood of the sin offering of atonement once in the year he shall make atonement for it throughout your generations. It is most holy to YHWH."

TABERNACLE MAZE

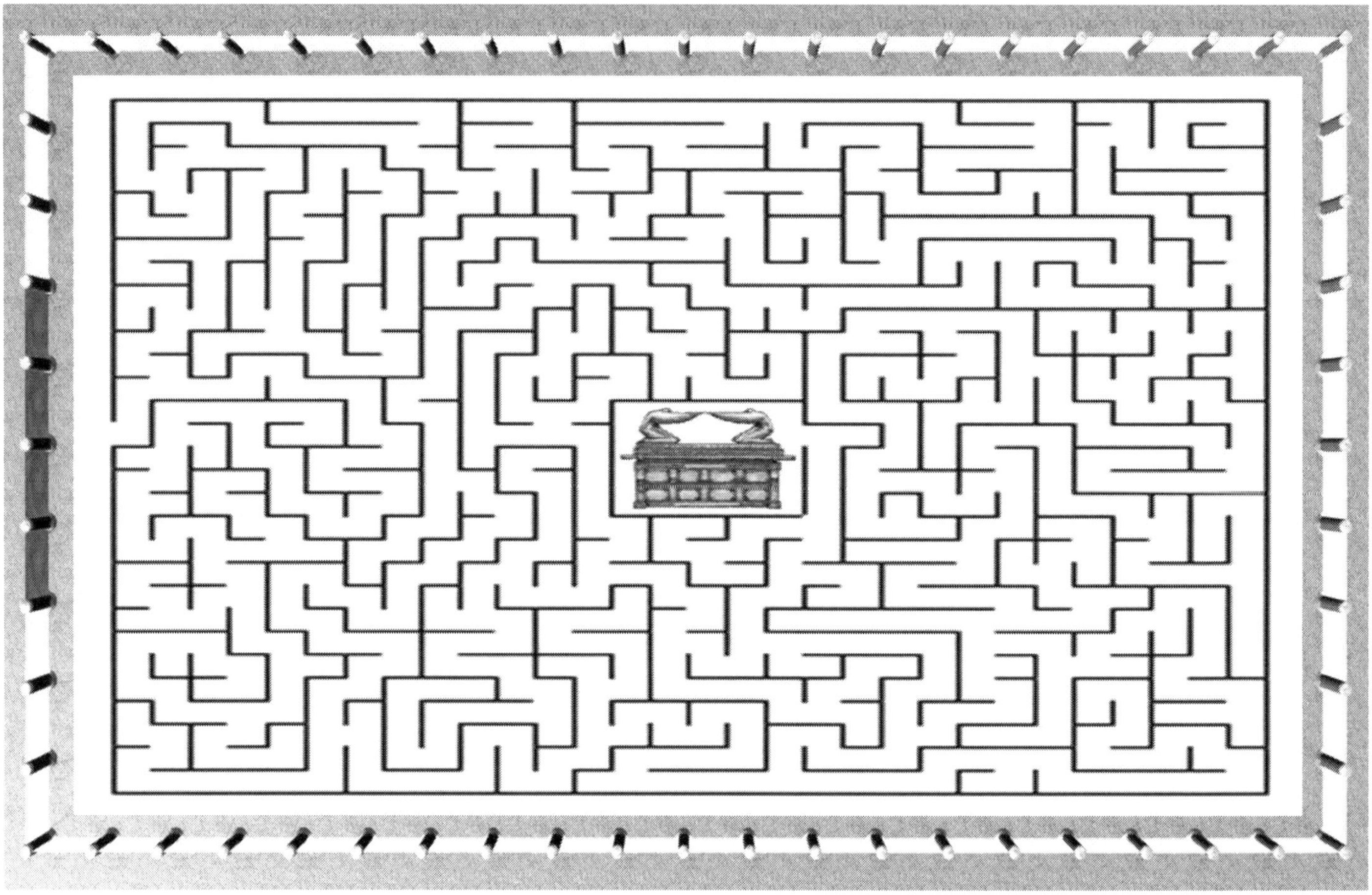

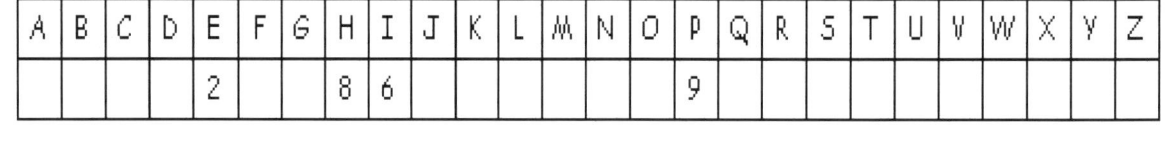

CRYPTOGRAM – EXODUS 29:45

A	B	C	D	E	F	G	H	I	J	K	L	M	N	O	P	Q	R	S	T	U	V	W	X	Y	Z
				2			8	6							9										

```
_I_  _I_   ___  _E_  ___   ___  ___  ___  ___   _H_ _E_   _P_ _E_  _P_  _E_
 6   14 6  18 18  24 14 2  18 18   17 23 20 19 13   5 8 2   9 2 20 9 18 2

    _I_  _E_          _I_           _E_   _H_ _E_ _I_
20 1  6 15 11 17 2 18  17 19 24  14 6 18 18   4 2   5 8 2 6 11

         ___
        13 20 24
```

page 98

KI TISA

כִּי תִשָּׂא

EXODUS

It Means: **When You Elevate**

Our Twenty First Torah Portion is called Ki Tisa! כִּי תִשָּׂא

Exodus 30:11 – Exodus 34:35

PROPHETS: 1 Kings 18:1-39
NEW TESTAMENT: Luke 11:14-20; Acts 7:35-8:1; 1 Corinthians 10:1-14; 2 Corinthians 3:1-18; Hebrews 9:1-14; Revelation 11

MAKE A MARK

Each time you hear someone say one of the words below make a '/" beside the word. See how many marks you can get!

heart	
plagues	
blood	
people	
hard	
Israelite	

FIRST FIND

~

If someone mentions a verse or scripture that is NOT in this Torah Portion, see if YOU can be the First to Find it!

The Census Tax

<u>SUNDAY</u> Exo 30:11 YHWH spoke to Moses, saying,

Exo 30:12 "When you take a census of the children of Israel, according to those who are counted among them, then each man shall give a ransom for his soul to YHWH, when you count them; that there be no plague among them when you count them.

Exo 30:13 They shall give this, everyone who passes over to those who are counted, half a shekel after the shekel of the sanctuary (the shekel is twenty gerahs); half a shekel for an offering to YHWH.

Exo 30:14 Everyone who passes over to those who are counted, from twenty years old and upward, shall give the offering to YHWH.

Exo 30:15 The rich shall not give more, and the poor shall not give less, than the half shekel, when they give the offering of YHWH, to make atonement for your souls.

Exo 30:16 **You shall take the atonement money from the children of Israel, and shall appoint it for the service of the Tent of Meeting; that it may be a memorial for the children of Israel before YHWH, to make atonement for your souls."**

The Bronze Basin

Exo 30:17 YHWH spoke to Moses, saying,

Exo 30:18 "You shall also make a basin of brass, and its base of brass, in which to wash. You shall put it between the Tent of Meeting and the altar, and you shall put water in it.

Exo 30:19 Aaron and his sons shall wash their hands and their feet in it.

Exo 30:20 When they go into the Tent of Meeting, they shall wash with water, that they not die; or when they come near to the altar to minister, to burn an offering made by fire to YHWH.

Exo 30:21 So they shall wash their hands and their feet, that they not die: and it shall be a statute forever to them, even to him and to his descendants throughout their generations."

The Anointing Oil and Incense

Exo 30:22 Moreover YHWH spoke to Moses, saying,

Exo 30:23 "Also take fine spices: of liquid myrrh, five hundred shekels; and of fragrant cinnamon half as much, even two hundred and fifty; and of fragrant cane, two hundred and fifty;

Exo 30:24 and of cassia five hundred, after the shekel of the sanctuary; and a hin of olive oil.

Exo 30:25 You shall make it into a holy anointing oil, a perfume compounded after the art of the perfumer: it shall be a holy anointing oil.

Exo 30:26 You shall use it to anoint the Tent of Meeting, the ark of the testimony,

Exo 30:27 the table and all its articles, the lamp stand and its accessories, the altar of incense,

Exo 30:28 the altar of burnt offering with all its utensils, and the basin with its base.

Exo 30:29 You shall sanctify them, that they may be most holy. Whatever touches them shall be holy.

Exo 30:30 You shall anoint Aaron and his sons, and sanctify them, that they may minister to me in the priest's office.

Exo 30:31 You shall speak to the children of Israel, saying, 'This shall be a holy anointing oil to me throughout your generations.

Exo 30:32 It shall not be poured on man's flesh, and do not make any like it, according to its composition. It is holy. It shall be holy to you.

Exo 30:33 Whoever compounds any like it, or whoever puts any of it on a stranger, he shall be cut off from his people.'"

Exo 30:34 YHWH said to Moses, "Take to yourself sweet spices, gum resin, and onycha, and galbanum; sweet spices with pure frankincense: there shall be an equal weight of each;

Exo 30:35 and you shall make incense of it, a perfume after the art of the perfumer, seasoned with salt, pure and holy:

Exo 30:36 and you shall beat some of it very small, and put some of it before the testimony in the Tent of Meeting, where I will meet with you. It shall be to you most holy.

Exo 30:37 The incense which you shall make, according to its composition you shall not make for yourselves: it shall be to you holy for YHWH.

Exo 30:38 Whoever shall make any like that, to smell of it, he shall be cut off from his people."

Oholiab and Bezalel

Exo 31:1 YHWH spoke to Moses, saying,

Exo 31:2 "Behold, I have called by name Bezalel the son of Uri, the son of Hur, of the tribe of Judah:

Exo 31:3 and I have filled him with the Spirit of God, in wisdom, and in understanding, and in knowledge, and in all kinds of workmanship,

Exo 31:4 to devise skillful works, to work in gold, and in silver, and in brass,

Exo 31:5 and in cutting of stones for setting, and in carving of wood, to work in all kinds of workmanship.

Exo 31:6 Behold, I myself have appointed with him Oholiab, the son of Ahisamach, of the tribe of Dan; and in the heart of all who are wise-hearted I have put wisdom, that they may make all that I have commanded you:

Exo 31:7 the Tent of Meeting, the ark of the testimony, the mercy seat that is on it, all the furniture of the Tent,

Exo 31:8 the table and its vessels, the pure lamp stand with all its vessels, the altar of incense,

Exo 31:9 the altar of burnt offering with all its vessels, the basin and its base,

Exo 31:10 the finely worked garments—the holy garments for Aaron the priest—the garments of his sons to minister in the priest's office,

Exo 31:11 the anointing oil, and the incense of sweet spices for the holy place: according to all that I have commanded you they shall do."

The Sabbath

Exo 31:12 YHWH spoke to Moses, saying,

Exo 31:13 "Speak also to the children of Israel, saying, 'Most certainly you shall keep my Sabbaths: for it is a sign between me and you throughout your generations; that you may know that I am YHWH who sanctifies you.

Exo 31:14 You shall keep the Sabbath therefore; for it is holy to you. Everyone who profanes it shall surely be put to death; for whoever does any work therein, that soul shall be cut off from among his people.

Exo 31:15 Six days shall work be done, but on the seventh day is a Sabbath of solemn rest, holy to YHWH. Whoever does any work on the Sabbath day shall surely be put to death.

Exo 31:16 Therefore the children of Israel shall keep the Sabbath, to observe the Sabbath throughout their generations, for a perpetual covenant.

Exo 31:17 It is a sign between me and the children of Israel forever; for in six days YHWH made heaven and earth, and on the seventh day he rested, and was refreshed.'"

Exo 31:18 **He gave to Moses, when he finished speaking with him on Mount Sinai, the two tablets of the testimony, stone tablets, written with God's finger.**

The Golden Calf

MONDAY Exo 32:1 When the people saw that Moses delayed to come down from the mountain, the people gathered themselves together to Aaron, and said to him, "Come, make us gods, which shall go before us; for as for this Moses, the man who brought us up out of the land of Egypt, we don't know what has become of him."

Exo 32:2 Aaron said to them, "Take off the golden rings, which are in the ears of your wives, of your sons, and of your daughters, and bring them to me."

Exo 32:3 **All the people took off the golden rings which were in their ears, and brought them to Aaron.**

Exo 32:4 He received what they handed him, fashioned it with an engraving tool, and made it a molten calf. Then they said, "These are your gods, Israel, which brought you up out of the land of Egypt."

Exo 32:5 When Aaron saw this, he built an altar before it; and Aaron made a proclamation, and said, "Tomorrow shall be a feast to YHWH."

Exo 32:6 They rose up early on the next day, and offered burnt offerings, and brought peace offerings; and the people sat down to eat and to drink, and rose up to play.

Exo 32:7 YHWH spoke to Moses, "Go, get down; for your people, who you brought up out of the land of Egypt, have corrupted themselves!

Exo 32:8 They have turned away quickly out of the way which I commanded them. They have made themselves a molten calf, and have worshiped it, and have sacrificed to it, and said, 'These are your gods, Israel, which brought you up out of the land of Egypt.'"

Exo 32:9 YHWH said to Moses, "I have seen these people, and behold, they are a stiff-necked people.

Exo 32:10 Now therefore leave me alone, that my wrath may burn hot against them, and that I may consume them; and I will make of you a great nation."

Exo 32:11 Moses begged YHWH his God, and said, "YHWH, why does your wrath burn hot against your people, that you have brought out of the land of Egypt with great power and with a mighty hand?

Exo 32:12 Why should the Egyptians speak, saying, 'He brought them out for evil, to kill them in the mountains, and to consume them from the surface of the earth?' Turn from your fierce wrath, and repent of this evil against your people.

Exo 32:13 Remember Abraham, Isaac, and Israel, your servants, to whom you swore by your own self, and said to them, 'I will multiply your offspring as the stars of the sky, and all this land that I have spoken of I will give to your offspring, and they shall inherit it forever.'"

Exo 32:14 YHWH repented of the evil which he said he would do to his people.

MY NOTES

Exo 32:15 Moses turned, and went down from the mountain, with the two tablets of the testimony in his hand; tablets that were written on both their sides; on the one side and on the other they were written.

Exo 32:16 The tablets were the work of God, and the writing was the writing of God, engraved on the tablets.

Exo 32:17 When Joshua heard the noise of the people as they shouted, he said to Moses, "There is the noise of war in the camp."

Exo 32:18 He said, "It isn't the voice of those who shout for victory. It is not the voice of those who cry for being overcome; but the noise of those who sing that I hear."

Exo 32:19 As soon as he came near to the camp, he saw the calf and the dancing. Then Moses' anger grew hot, and he threw the tablets out of his hands, and broke them beneath the mountain.

Exo 32:20 He took the calf which they had made, and burned it with fire, ground it to powder, and scattered it on the water, and made the children of Israel drink it.

Exo 32:21 Moses said to Aaron, "What did these people do to you, that you have brought a great sin on them?"

Exo 32:22 Aaron said, "Don't let the anger of my lord grow hot. You know the people, that they are set on evil.

Exo 32:23 For they said to me, 'Make us gods, which shall go before us. As for this Moses, the man who brought us up out of the land of Egypt, we don't know what has become of him.'

Exo 32:24 I said to them, 'Whoever has any gold, let them take it off:' so they gave it to me; and I threw it into the fire, and out came this calf."

Exo 32:25 When Moses saw that the people had broken loose, (for Aaron had let them loose for a derision among their enemies),

Exo 32:26 then Moses stood in the gate of the camp, and said, "Whoever is on YHWH's side, come to me!" All the sons of Levi gathered themselves together to him.

Exo 32:27 He said to them, "YHWH says, the God of Israel, 'Every man put his sword on his thigh, and go back and forth from gate to gate throughout the camp, and every man kill his brother, and every man his companion, and every man his neighbor.'"

Exo 32:28 The sons of Levi did according to the word of Moses: and there fell of the people that day about three thousand men.

Exo 32:29 Moses said, "Consecrate yourselves today to YHWH, yes, every man against his son, and against his brother; that he may give you a blessing today."

Exo 32:30 On the next day, Moses said to the people, "You have sinned a great sin. Now I will go up to YHWH. Perhaps I shall make atonement for your sin."

Exo 32:31 Moses returned to YHWH, and said, "Oh, this people have sinned a great sin, and have made themselves gods of gold.

Exo 32:32 Yet now, if you will, forgive their sin—and if not, please blot me out of your book which you have written."

Exo 32:33 YHWH said to Moses, "Whoever has sinned against me, him I will blot out of my book.

Exo 32:34 Now go, lead the people to the place of which I have spoken to you. Behold, my angel shall go before you. Nevertheless in the day when I punish, I will punish them for their sin."

Exo 32:35 YHWH struck the people, because they made the calf, which Aaron made.

The Command to Leave Sinai

Exo 33:1 YHWH spoke to Moses, "Depart, go up from here, you and the people that you have brought up out of the land of Egypt, to the land of which I swore to Abraham, to Isaac, and to Jacob, saying, 'I will give it to your offspring.'

Exo 33:2 I will send an angel before you; and I will drive out the Canaanite, the Amorite, and the Hittite, and the Perizzite, the Hivite, and the Jebusite:

Exo 33:3 to a land flowing with milk and honey: for I will not go up among you, for you are a stiff-necked people, lest I consume you on the way."

Exo 33:4 When the people heard this evil news, they mourned: and no one put on his jewelry.

Exo 33:5 YHWH said to Moses, "Tell the children of Israel, 'You are a stiff-necked people. If I were to go up among you for one moment, I would consume you. Therefore now take off your jewelry from you, that I may know what to do to you.'"

Exo 33:6 ***The children of Israel stripped themselves of their jewelry from Mount Horeb onward.***

The Tent of Meeting

Exo 33:7 Now Moses used to take the tent and pitch it outside the camp, far away from the camp, and he called it "The Tent of Meeting." Everyone who sought YHWH went out to the Tent of Meeting, which was outside the camp.

Exo 33:8 When Moses went out to the Tent, all the people rose up, and stood, everyone at their tent door, and watched Moses, until he had gone into the Tent.

Exo 33:9 When Moses entered into the Tent, the pillar of cloud descended, stood at the door of the Tent, and spoke with Moses.

Exo 33:10 All the people saw the pillar of cloud stand at the door of the Tent, and all the people rose up and worshiped, everyone at their tent door.

Exo 33:11 YHWH spoke to Moses face to face, as a man speaks to his friend. He turned again into the camp, but his servant Joshua, the son of Nun, a young man, didn't depart from the Tent.

Moses' Intercession

TUESDAY Exo 33:12 Moses said to YHWH, "Behold, you tell me, 'Bring up this people:' and you haven't let me know whom you will send with me. Yet you have said, 'I know you by name, and you have also found favor in my sight.'

Exo 33:13 **Now therefore, if I have found favor in your sight, please show me now your way, that I may know you, so that I may find favor in your sight: and consider that this nation is your people."**

Exo 33:14 He said, "My presence will go with you, and I will give you rest."

Exo 33:15 He said to him, "If your presence doesn't go with me, don't carry us up from here.

Exo 33:16 For how would people know that I have found favor in your sight, I and your people? Isn't it that you go with us, so that we are separated, I and your people, from all the people who are on the surface of the earth?"

WEDNESDAY Exo 33:17 YHWH said to Moses, "I will do this thing also that you have spoken; for you have found favor in my sight, and I know you by name."

Exo 33:18 He said, "Please show me your glory."

Exo 33:19 **He said, "I will make all my goodness pass before you, and will proclaim YHWH's name before you. I will be gracious to whom I will be gracious, and will show mercy on whom I will show mercy."**

Exo 33:20 He said, "You cannot see my face, for man may not see me and live."

Exo 33:21 YHWH also said, "Behold, there is a place by me, and you shall stand on the rock.

Exo 33:22 It will happen, while my glory passes by, that I will put you in a cleft of the rock, and will cover you with my hand until I have passed by;

Exo 33:23 then I will take away my hand, and you will see my back; but my face shall not be seen."

Moses Makes New Tablets

THURSDAY Exo 34:1 YHWH said to Moses, "Chisel two stone tablets like the first. I will write on the tablets the words that were on the first tablets, which you broke.

Exo 34:2 Be ready by the morning, and come up in the morning to Mount Sinai, and present yourself there to me on the top of the mountain.

Exo 34:3 No one shall come up with you or be seen anywhere on the mountain. Do not let the flocks or herds graze in front of that mountain."

Exo 34:4 He chiseled two tablets of stone like the first; and Moses rose up early in the morning, and went up to Mount Sinai, as YHWH had commanded him, and took in his hand two stone tablets.

Exo 34:5 YHWH descended in the cloud, and stood with him there, and proclaimed YHWH's name.

Exo 34:6 **YHWH passed by before him, and proclaimed, "YHWH! YHWH, a merciful and gracious God, slow to anger, and abundant in loving kindness and truth,**

Exo 34:7 keeping loving kindness for thousands, forgiving iniquity and disobedience and sin; and who will by no means clear the guilty, visiting the iniquity of the fathers on the children, and on the children's children, on the third and on the fourth generation."

Exo 34:8 Moses hurried and bowed his head toward the earth, and worshiped.

Exo 34:9 He said, "If now I have found favor in your sight, Lord, please let the Lord go among us; although this is a stiff-necked people; pardon our iniquity and our sin, and take us for your inheritance."

The Covenant Renewed

FRIDAY Exo 34:10 He said, "Behold, I make a covenant: before all your people I will do marvels, such as have not been worked in all the earth, nor in any nation; and all the people among which you are shall see the work of YHWH; for it is an awesome thing that I do with you.

Exo 34:11 Observe that which I command you today. Behold, I drive out before you the Amorite, the Canaanite, the Hittite, the Perizzite, the Hivite, and the Jebusite.

Exo 34:12 Be careful, lest you make a covenant with the inhabitants of the land where you are going, lest it be for a snare among you:

Exo 34:13 but you shall break down their altars, and dash in pieces their pillars, and you shall cut down their Asherah poles;

Exo 34:14 for you shall worship no other god: for YHWH, whose name is Jealous, is a jealous God.

Exo 34:15 "Don't make a covenant with the inhabitants of the land, lest they play the prostitute after their gods, and sacrifice to their gods, and one call you and you eat of his sacrifice;

Exo 34:16 and you take of their daughters to your sons, and their daughters play the prostitute after their gods, and make your sons play the prostitute after their gods.

Exo 34:17 "You shall make no cast idols for yourselves.

Exo 34:18 ***"You shall keep the feast of unleavened bread. Seven days you shall eat unleavened bread, as I commanded you, at the time appointed in the month Abib; for in the month Abib you came out of Egypt.***

Exo 34:19 "All that opens the womb is mine; and all your livestock that is male, the firstborn of cow and sheep.

Exo 34:20 You shall redeem the firstborn of a donkey with a lamb. If you will not redeem it, then you shall break its neck. You shall redeem all the firstborn of your sons. No one shall appear before me empty.

Exo 34:21 "Six days you shall work, but on the seventh day you shall rest: in plowing time and in harvest you shall rest.

Exo 34:22 "You shall observe the feast of weeks with the first fruits of wheat harvest, and the feast of harvest at the year's end.

Exo 34:23 Three times in the year all your males shall appear before the Lord YHWH, the God of Israel.

Exo 34:24 For I will drive out nations before you and enlarge your borders; neither shall any man desire your land when you go up to appear before YHWH, your God, three times in the year.

Exo 34:25 "You shall not offer the blood of my sacrifice with leavened bread. The sacrifice of the feast of the Passover shall not be left to the morning.

Exo 34:26 "You shall bring the first of the first fruits of your ground to the house of YHWH your God. "You shall not boil a young goat in its mother's milk."

SABBATH Exo 34:27 YHWH said to Moses, "Write you these words: for in accordance with these words I have made a covenant with you and with Israel."

Exo 34:28 He was there with YHWH forty days and forty nights; he neither ate bread, nor drank water. He wrote on the tablets the words of the covenant, the ten commandments.

The Shining Face of Moses

Exo 34:29 When Moses came down from Mount Sinai with the two tablets of the testimony in Moses' hand, when he came down from the mountain, Moses didn't know that the skin of his face shone by reason of his speaking with him.

Exo 34:30 When Aaron and all the children of Israel saw Moses, behold, the skin of his face shone; and they were afraid to come near him.

Exo 34:31 Moses called to them, and Aaron and all the rulers of the congregation returned to him; and Moses spoke to them.

Exo 34:32 Afterward all the children of Israel came near, and he gave them all the commandments that YHWH had spoken with him on Mount Sinai.

Exo 34:33 **When Moses was done speaking with them, he put a veil on his face.**

Exo 34:34 But when Moses went in before YHWH to speak with him, he took the veil off, until he came out; and he came out, and spoke to the children of Israel that which he was commanded.

Exo 34:35 The children of Israel saw Moses' face, that the skin of Moses' face shone: and Moses put the veil on his face again, until he went in to speak with him.

KI TISA WORDFIND

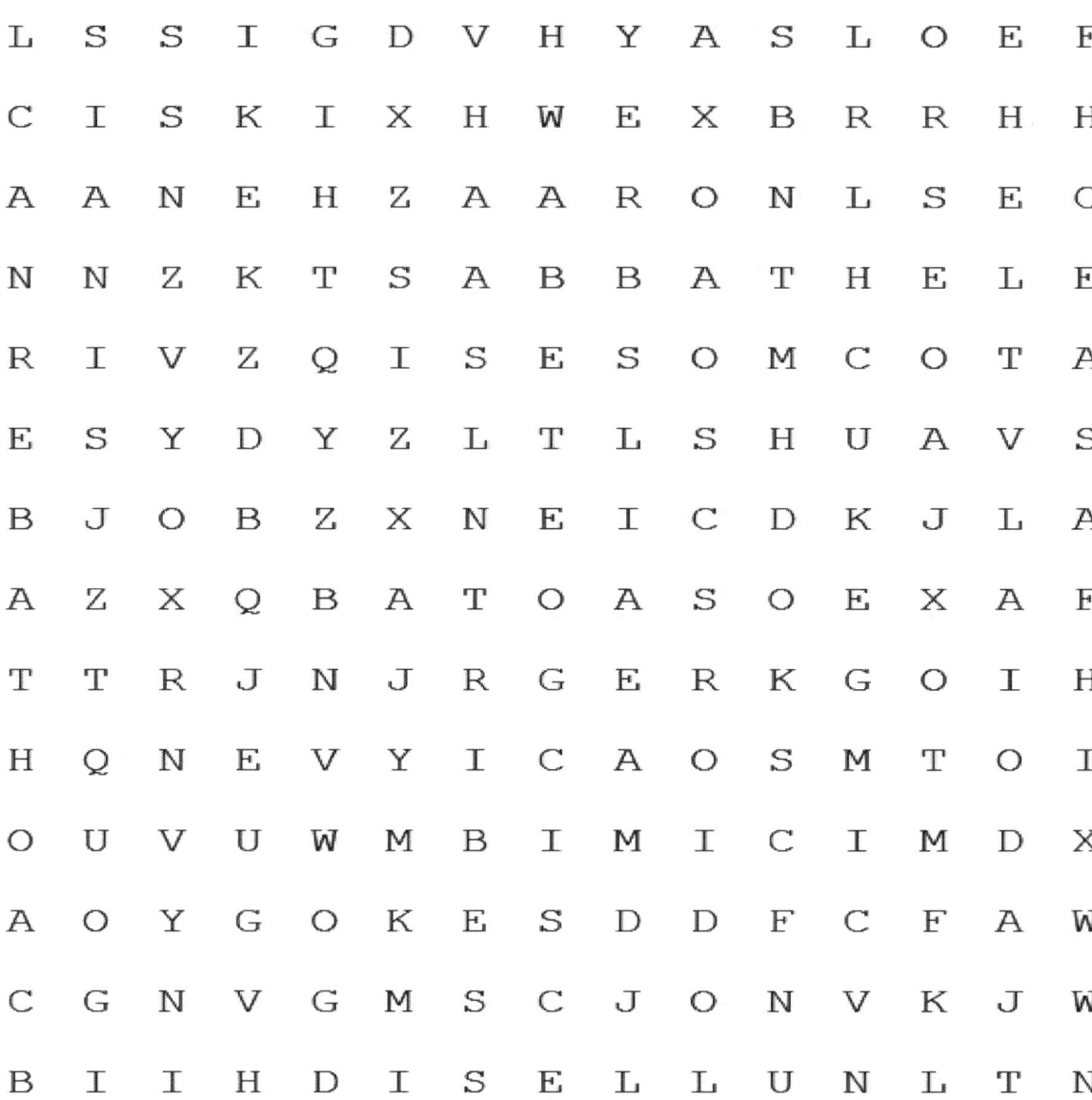

L	S	S	I	G	D	V	H	Y	A	S	L	O	E	F
C	I	S	K	I	X	H	W	E	X	B	R	R	H	H
A	A	N	E	H	Z	A	A	R	O	N	L	S	E	C
N	N	Z	K	T	S	A	B	B	A	T	H	E	L	E
R	I	V	Z	Q	I	S	E	S	O	M	C	O	T	A
E	S	Y	D	Y	Z	L	T	L	S	H	U	A	V	S
B	J	O	B	Z	X	N	E	I	C	D	K	J	L	A
A	Z	X	Q	B	A	T	O	A	S	O	E	X	A	F
T	T	R	J	N	J	R	G	E	R	K	G	O	I	H
H	Q	N	E	V	Y	I	C	A	O	S	M	T	O	I
O	U	V	U	W	M	B	I	M	I	C	I	M	D	X
A	O	Y	G	O	K	E	S	D	D	F	C	F	A	W
C	G	N	V	G	M	S	C	J	O	N	V	K	J	W
B	I	I	H	D	I	S	E	L	L	U	N	L	T	N

AARON	ISRAELITES	SABBATH
CALF	MOSES	SMOKE
CLOUDS	MOUNT	TABERNACLE
COVENANT	SINAI	TABLETS
IDOL		TRIBES

BONUS: FILL IN THE BLANKS

EXODUS 31:13 "You are to speak to the _____ ____ _____ and say, 'Above all you shall keep my _____, for this is a _____ between me and you throughout your _____, that you may know that I, the Lord, sanctify you.

page 112

VAYAKHEL

וַיַּקְהֵל

EXODUS

It Means: **And He Assembled**

Our Twenty Second Torah Portion is called Vayakhel! וַיַּקְהֵל
Exodus 35:1 – Exodus 38:20
PROPHETS: Ezekiel 36:16-381
NEW TESTAMENT: 2 Corinthians 8:1-9:15

MAKE A MARK

Each time you hear someone say one of the words below make a '/" beside the word. See how many marks you can get!

heart	
plagues	
blood	
people	
hard	
Israelites	

FIRST FIND

~

If someone mentions a verse or scripture that is NOT in this Torah Portion, see if YOU can be the First to Find it!

HOW MANY CAN YOU NAME?

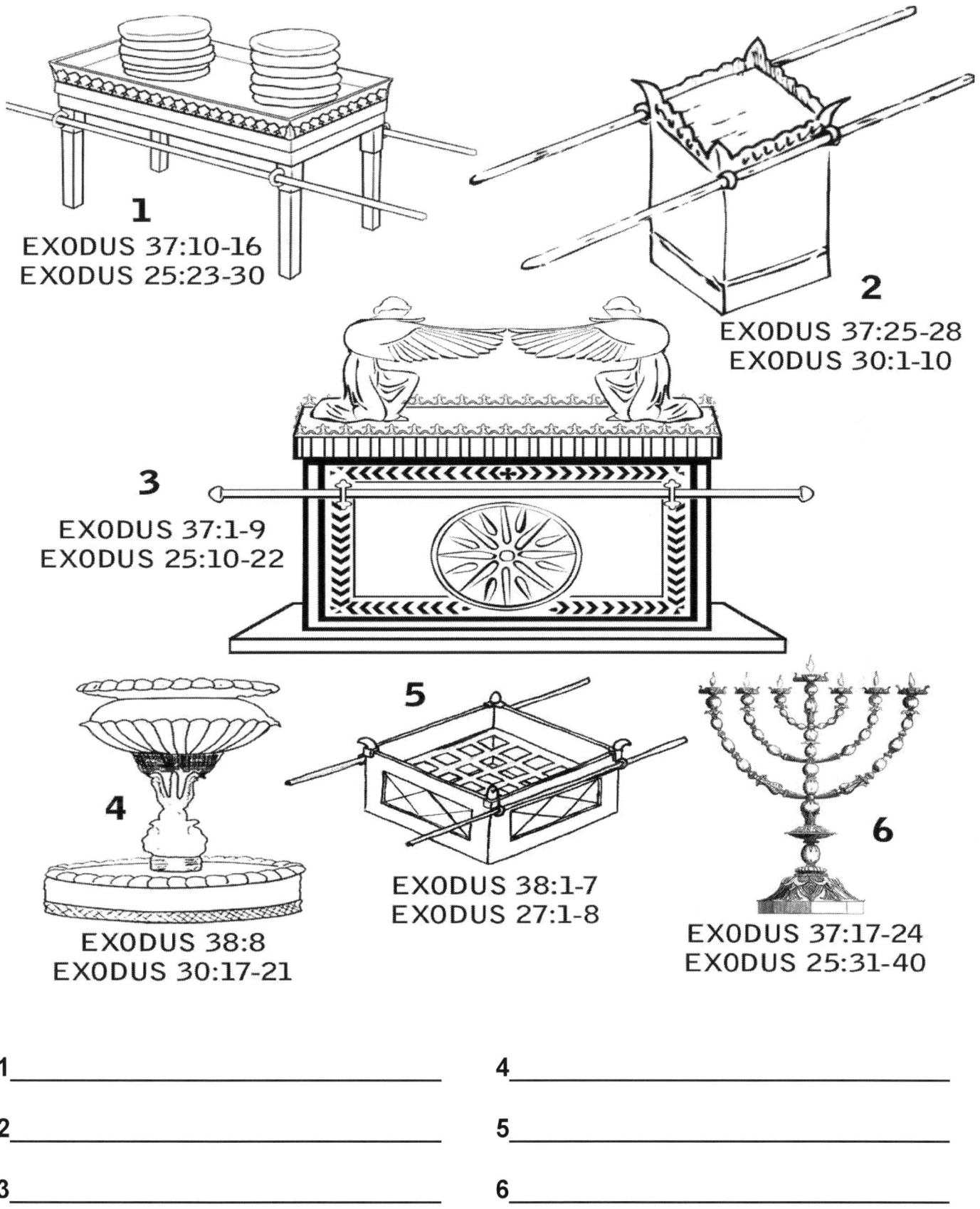

1 EXODUS 37:10-16 / EXODUS 25:23-30

2 EXODUS 37:25-28 / EXODUS 30:1-10

3 EXODUS 37:1-9 / EXODUS 25:10-22

4 EXODUS 38:8 / EXODUS 30:17-21

5 EXODUS 38:1-7 / EXODUS 27:1-8

6 EXODUS 37:17-24 / EXODUS 25:31-40

1 _____ 4 _____

2 _____ 5 _____

3 _____ 6 _____

Sabbath Regulations

<u>SUNDAY</u> Exo 35:1 Moses assembled all the congregation of the children of Israel, and said to them, "These are the words which YHWH has commanded, that you should do them.

Exo 35:2 'Six days shall work be done, but on the seventh day there shall be a holy day for you, a Sabbath of solemn rest to YHWH: whoever does any work in it shall be put to death.

Exo 35:3 You shall kindle no fire throughout your habitations on the Sabbath day.'"

Contributions for the Tabernacle

Exo 35:4 Moses spoke to all the congregation of the children of Israel, saying, "This is the thing which YHWH commanded, saying,

Exo 35:5 **'Take from among you an offering to YHWH. Whoever is of a willing heart, let him bring it, YHWH's offering: gold, silver, brass,**

Exo 35:6 blue, purple, scarlet, fine linen, goats' hair,

Exo 35:7 rams' skins dyed red, sea cow hides, acacia wood,

Exo 35:8 oil for the light, spices for the anointing oil and for the sweet incense,

Exo 35:9 onyx stones, and stones to be set for the ephod and for the breastplate.

Exo 35:10 "'Let every wise-hearted man among you come, and make all that YHWH has commanded:

Exo 35:11 the tabernacle, its outer covering, its roof, its clasps, its boards, its bars, its pillars, and its sockets;

Exo 35:12 the ark, and its poles, the mercy seat, the veil of the screen;

Exo 35:13 the table with its poles and all its vessels, and the show bread;

Exo 35:14 the lamp stand also for the light, with its vessels, its lamps, and the oil for the light;

Exo 35:15 and the altar of incense with its poles, the anointing oil, the sweet incense, the screen for the door, at the door of the tabernacle;

Exo 35:16 the altar of burnt offering, with its grating of brass, it poles, and all its vessels, the basin and its base;

Exo 35:17 the hangings of the court, its pillars, their sockets, and the screen for the gate of the court;

Exo 35:18 the pins of the tabernacle, the pins of the court, and their cords;

Exo 35:19 the finely worked garments, for ministering in the holy place, the holy garments for Aaron the priest, and the garments of his sons, to minister in the priest's office.'"

Exo 35:20 All the congregation of the children of Israel departed from the presence of Moses.

MONDAY Exo 35:21 They came, everyone whose heart stirred him up, and everyone whom his spirit made willing, and brought YHWH's offering, for the work of the Tent of Meeting, and for all of its service, and for the holy garments.

Exo 35:22 They came, both men and women, as many as were willing-hearted, and brought brooches, earrings, signet rings, and armlets, all jewels of gold; even every man who offered an offering of gold to YHWH.

Exo 35:23 Everyone, with whom was found blue, purple, scarlet, fine linen, goats' hair, rams' skins dyed red, and sea cow hides, brought them.

Exo 35:24 Everyone who offered an offering of silver and brass brought YHWH's offering; and everyone, with whom was found acacia wood for any work of the service, brought it.

Exo 35:25 All the women who were wise-hearted spun with their hands, and brought that which they had spun, the blue, the purple, the scarlet, and the fine linen.

Exo 35:26 All the women whose heart stirred them up in wisdom spun the goats' hair.

Exo 35:27 The rulers brought the onyx stones and the stones to be set for the ephod and for the breastplate;

Exo 35:28 with the spice and the oil for the light, for the anointing oil, and for the sweet incense.

Exo 35:29 ***The children of Israel brought a freewill offering to YHWH; every man and woman, whose heart made them willing to bring for all the work, which YHWH had commanded to be made by Moses.***

Construction of the Tabernacle

TUESDAY Exo 35:30 Moses said to the children of Israel, "Behold, YHWH has called by name Bezalel the son of Uri, the son of Hur, of the tribe of Judah.

Exo 35:31 ***He has filled him with the Spirit of God, in wisdom, in understanding, in knowledge, and in all kinds of workmanship;***

Exo 35:32 and to make skillful works, to work in gold, in silver, in brass,

Exo 35:33 in cutting of stones for setting, and in carving of wood, to work in all kinds of skillful workmanship.

Exo 35:34 He has put in his heart that he may teach, both he, and Oholiab, the son of Ahisamach, of the tribe of Dan.

Exo 35:35 He has filled them with wisdom of heart, to work all kinds of workmanship, of the engraver, of the skillful workman, and of the embroiderer, in blue, in purple, in scarlet, and in fine linen, and of the weaver, even of those who do any workmanship, and of those who make skillful works.

Exo 36:1 "Bezalel and Oholiab shall work with every wise-hearted man, in whom YHWH has put wisdom and understanding to know how to do all the work for the service of the sanctuary, according to all that YHWH has commanded."

Exo 36:2 Moses called Bezalel and Oholiab, and every wise-hearted man, in whose heart YHWH had put wisdom, even everyone whose heart stirred him up to come to the work to do it:

Exo 36:3 and they received from Moses all the offering which the children of Israel had brought for the work of the service of the sanctuary, with which to make it. They brought yet to him freewill offerings every morning.

Exo 36:4 All the wise men, who performed all the work of the sanctuary, each came from his work which they did.

Exo 36:5 They spoke to Moses, saying, "The people bring much more than enough for the service of the work which YHWH commanded to make."

Exo 36:6 Moses gave commandment, and they caused it to be proclaimed throughout the camp, saying, "Let neither man nor woman make anything else for the offering for the sanctuary." So the people were restrained from bringing.

Exo 36:7 For the stuff they had was sufficient for all the work to make it, and too much.

WEDNESDAY Exo 36:8 *All the wise-hearted men among those who did the work made the tabernacle with ten curtains; of fine twined linen, blue, purple, and scarlet, with cherubim, the work of the skillful workman, they made them.*

Exo 36:9 The length of each curtain was twenty-eight cubits, and the width of each curtain four cubits. All the curtains had one measure.

Exo 36:10 He coupled five curtains to one another, and the other five curtains he coupled to one another.

Exo 36:11 He made loops of blue on the edge of the one curtain from the edge in the coupling. Likewise he made in the edge of the curtain that was outermost in the second coupling.

Exo 36:12 He made fifty loops in the one curtain, and he made fifty loops in the edge of the curtain that was in the second coupling. The loops were opposite to one another.

Exo 36:13 He made fifty clasps of gold, and coupled the curtains to one another with the clasps: so the tabernacle was a unit.

Exo 36:14 He made curtains of goats' hair for a covering over the tabernacle. He made them eleven curtains.

Exo 36:15 The length of each curtain was thirty cubits, and four cubits the width of each curtain. The eleven curtains had one measure.

Exo 36:16 He coupled five curtains by themselves, and six curtains by themselves.

Exo 36:17 He made fifty loops on the edge of the curtain that was outermost in the coupling, and he made fifty loops on the edge of the curtain which was outermost in the second coupling.

Exo 36:18 He made fifty clasps of brass to couple the tent together, that it might be a unit.

Exo 36:19 He made a covering for the tent of rams' skins dyed red, and a covering of sea cow hides above.

THURSDAY Exo 36:20 He made the boards for the tabernacle of acacia wood, standing up.

Exo 36:21 Ten cubits was the length of a board, and a cubit and a half the width of each board.

Exo 36:22 Each board had two tenons, joined to one another. He made all the boards of the tabernacle this way.

Exo 36:23 He made the boards for the tabernacle: twenty boards for the south side southward.

Exo 36:24 He made forty sockets of silver under the twenty boards; two sockets under one board for its two tenons, and two sockets under another board for its two tenons.

Exo 36:25 For the second side of the tabernacle, on the north side, he made twenty boards,

Exo 36:26 and their forty sockets of silver; two sockets under one board, and two sockets under another board.

Exo 36:27 For the far part of the tabernacle westward he made six boards.

Exo 36:28 He made two boards for the corners of the tabernacle in the far part.

Exo 36:29 They were double beneath, and in the same way they were all the way to its top to one ring. He did this to both of them in the two corners.

Exo 36:30 There were eight boards, and their sockets of silver, sixteen sockets; under every board two sockets.

Exo 36:31 He made bars of acacia wood; five for the boards of the one side of the tabernacle,

Exo 36:32 and five bars for the boards of the other side of the tabernacle, and five bars for the boards of the tabernacle for the hinder part westward.

Exo 36:33 He made the middle bar to pass through in the middle of the boards from the one end to the other.

Exo 36:34 He overlaid the boards with gold, and made their rings of gold as places for the bars, and overlaid the bars with gold.

Exo 36:35 He made the veil of blue, purple, scarlet, and fine twined linen: with cherubim. He made it the work of a skillful workman.

Exo 36:36 He made four pillars of acacia for it, and overlaid them with gold. Their hooks were of gold. He cast four sockets of silver for them.

Exo 36:37 He made a screen for the door of the tent, of blue, purple, scarlet, and fine twined linen, the work of an embroiderer;

Exo 36:38 and the five pillars of it with their hooks. He overlaid their capitals and their fillets with gold, and their five sockets were of brass.

Making the Ark

Exo 37:1 **Bezalel made the ark of acacia wood. Its length was two and a half cubits, and its width a cubit and a half, and a cubit and a half its height.**

Exo 37:2 He overlaid it with pure gold inside and outside, and made a molding of gold for it around it.

Exo 37:3 He cast four rings of gold for it, in its four feet; even two rings on its one side, and two rings on its other side.

Exo 37:4 He made poles of acacia wood, and overlaid them with gold.

Exo 37:5 He put the poles into the rings on the sides of the ark, to bear the ark.

Exo 37:6 He made a mercy seat of pure gold. Its length was two and a half cubits, and a cubit and a half its width.

Exo 37:7 He made two cherubim of gold. He made them of beaten work, at the two ends of the mercy seat;

Exo 37:8 one cherub at the one end, and one cherub at the other end. He made the cherubim of one piece with the mercy seat at its two ends.

Exo 37:9 The cherubim spread out their wings on high, covering the mercy seat with their wings, with their faces toward one another. The faces of the cherubim were toward the mercy seat.

Making the Table

Exo 37:10 He made the table of acacia wood. Its length was two cubits, and its width was a cubit, and its height was a cubit and a half.

Exo 37:11 He overlaid it with pure gold, and made a gold molding around it.

Exo 37:12 He made a border of a hand width around it, and made a golden molding on its border around it.

Exo 37:13 He cast four rings of gold for it, and put the rings in the four corners that were on its four feet.

Exo 37:14 The rings were close by the border, the places for the poles to carry the table.

Exo 37:15 He made the poles of acacia wood, and overlaid them with gold, to carry the table.

Exo 37:16 He made the vessels which were on the table, its dishes, its spoons, its bowls, and its pitchers with which to pour out, of pure gold.

Making the Lampstand

FRIDAY Exo 37:17 He made the lamp stand of pure gold. He made the lamp stand of beaten work. Its base, its shaft, its cups, its buds, and its flowers were of one piece with it.

Exo 37:18 There were six branches going out of its sides: three branches of the lamp stand out of its one side, and three branches of the lamp stand out of its other side:

Exo 37:19 three cups made like almond blossoms in one branch, a bud and a flower, and three cups made like almond blossoms in the other branch, a bud and a flower: so for the six branches going out of the lamp stand.

Exo 37:20 In the lamp stand were four cups made like almond blossoms, its buds and its flowers;

Exo 37:21 and a bud under two branches of one piece with it, and a bud under two branches of one piece with it, and a bud under two branches of one piece with it, for the six branches going out of it.

Exo 37:22 **Their buds and their branches were of one piece with it. The whole thing was one beaten work of pure gold.**

Exo 37:23 He made its seven lamps, and its snuffers, and its snuff dishes, of pure gold.

Exo 37:24 He made it of a talent of pure gold, with all its vessels.

Making the Altar of Incense

Exo 37:25 He made the altar of incense of acacia wood. It was square: its length was a cubit, and its width a cubit. Its height was two cubits. Its horns were of one piece with it.

Exo 37:26 He overlaid it with pure gold, its top, its sides around it, and its horns. He made a gold molding around it.

Exo 37:27 He made two golden rings for it under its molding crown, on its two ribs, on its two sides, for places for poles with which to carry it.

Exo 37:28 He made the poles of acacia wood, and overlaid them with gold.

Exo 37:29 He made the holy anointing oil and the pure incense of sweet spices, after the art of the perfumer.

Making the Altar of Burnt Offering

SABBATH Exo 38:1 He made the altar of burnt offering of acacia wood. It was square. Its length was five cubits, its width was five cubits, and its height was three cubits.

Exo 38:2 He made its horns on its four corners. Its horns were of one piece with it, and he overlaid it with brass.

Exo 38:3 He made all the vessels of the altar, the pots, the shovels, the basins, the forks, and the fire pans. He made all its vessels of brass.

Exo 38:4 He made for the altar a grating of a network of brass, under the ledge around it beneath, reaching halfway up.

Exo 38:5 He cast four rings for the four ends of brass grating, to be places for the poles.

Exo 38:6 He made the poles of acacia wood, and overlaid them with brass.

Exo 38:7 He put the poles into the rings on the sides of the altar, with which to carry it. He made it hollow with planks.

Making the Bronze Basin

Exo 38:8 He made the basin of brass, and its base of brass, out of the mirrors of the ministering women who ministered at the door of the Tent of Meeting.

Making the Court

Exo 38:9 He made the court: for the south side southward the hangings of the court were of fine twined linen, one hundred cubits;

Exo 38:10 their pillars were twenty, and their sockets twenty, of brass; the hooks of the pillars and their fillets were of silver.

Exo 38:11 For the north side one hundred cubits, their pillars twenty, and their sockets twenty, of brass; the hooks of the pillars, and their fillets, of silver.

Exo 38:12 For the west side were hangings of fifty cubits, their pillars ten, and their sockets ten; the hooks of the pillars, and their fillets, of silver.

Exo 38:13 For the east side eastward fifty cubits.

Exo 38:14 The hangings for the one side were fifteen cubits; their pillars three, and their sockets three;

Exo 38:15 and so for the other side: on this hand and that hand by the gate of the court were hangings of fifteen cubits; their pillars three, and their sockets three.

Exo 38:16 All the hangings around the court were of fine twined linen.

Exo 38:17 The sockets for the pillars were of brass. The hooks of the pillars and their fillets were of silver; and the overlaying of their capitals, of silver; and all the pillars of the court were filleted with silver.

Exo 38:18 **The screen for the gate of the court was the work of the embroiderer, of blue, purple, scarlet, and fine twined linen. Twenty cubits was the length, and the height in the width was five cubits, like to the hangings of the court.**

Exo 38:19 Their pillars were four, and their sockets four, of brass; their hooks of silver, and the overlaying of their capitals, and their fillets, of silver.

Exo 38:20 All the pins of the tabernacle, and around the court, were of brass.

MY NOTES

KI TISA SCRAMBLE

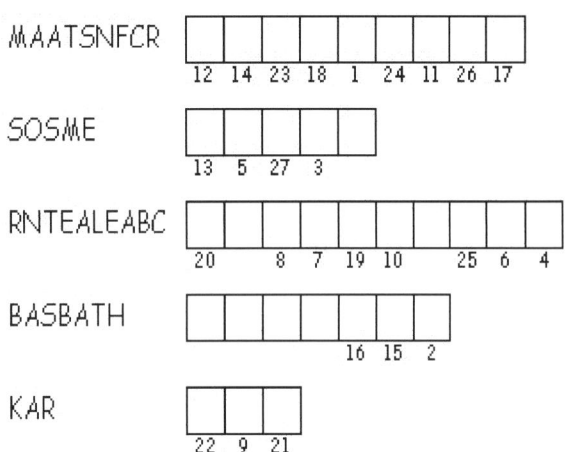

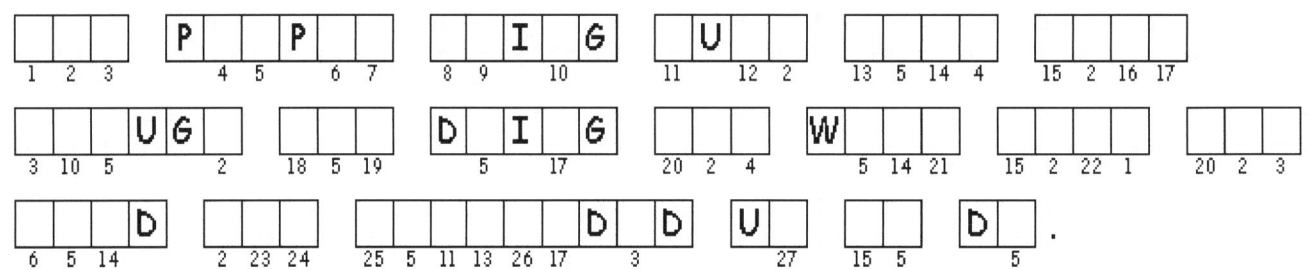

VERSE FIND – EXODUS 39:42

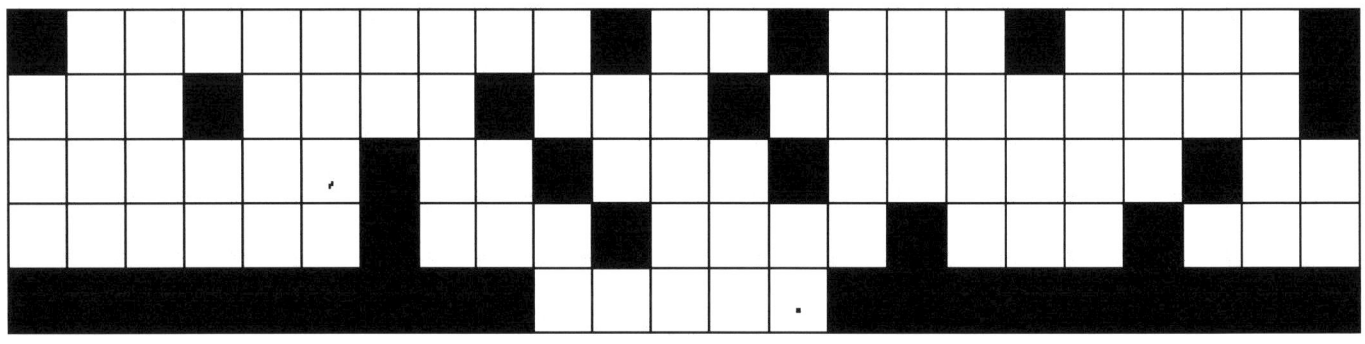

PEKUDEI

פְּקוּדֵי

EXODUS

It Means: **Accountings**

Our Twenty Third Torah Portion is called Pekudei! פְּקוּדֵי
Exodus 10:1 – Exodus 13:16
PROPHETS: Kings 7:13-50
NEW TESTAMENT: Hebrews 9:1-14; Revelation 11:1-13

MAKE A MARK

Each time you hear someone say one of the words below make a "✓" beside the word. See how many marks you can get!

heart	
plagues	
blood	
people	
hard	
Israelites	

FIRST FIND

~

If someone mentions a verse or scripture that is NOT in this Torah Portion, see if YOU can be the First to Find it!

Materials for the Tabernacle

<u>SUNDAY</u> Exo 38:21 *This is the amount of material used for the tabernacle, even the Tabernacle of the Testimony, as they were counted, according to the commandment of Moses, for the service of the Levites, by the hand of Ithamar, the son of Aaron the priest.*

Exo 38:22 Bezalel the son of Uri, the son of Hur, of the tribe of Judah, made all that YHWH commanded Moses.

Exo 38:23 With him was Oholiab, the son of Ahisamach, of the tribe of Dan, an engraver, and a skillful workman, and an embroiderer in blue, in purple, in scarlet, and in fine linen.

Exo 38:24 All the gold that was used for the work in all the work of the sanctuary, even the gold of the offering, was twenty-nine talents, and seven hundred thirty shekels, after the shekel of the sanctuary.

Exo 38:25 The silver of those who were counted of the congregation was one hundred talents, and one thousand seven hundred seventy-five shekels, after the shekel of the sanctuary:

Exo 38:26 a beka a head, that is, half a shekel, after the shekel of the sanctuary, for everyone who passed over to those who were counted, from twenty years old and upward, for six hundred three thousand five hundred fifty men.

Exo 38:27 The one hundred talents of silver were for casting the sockets of the sanctuary, and the sockets of the veil; one hundred sockets for the one hundred talents, a talent for a socket.

Exo 38:28 Of the one thousand seven hundred seventy-five shekels he made hooks for the pillars, overlaid their capitals, and made fillets for them.

Exo 38:29 The brass of the offering was seventy talents, and two thousand four hundred shekels.

Exo 38:30 With this he made the sockets to the door of the Tent of Meeting, the bronze altar, the bronze grating for it, all the vessels of the altar,

Exo 38:31 the sockets around the court, the sockets of the gate of the court, all the pins of the tabernacle, and all the pins around the court.

Making the Priestly Garments

Exo 39:1 Of the blue, purple, and scarlet, they made finely worked garments, for ministering in the holy place, and made the holy garments for Aaron; as YHWH commanded Moses.

<u>MONDAY</u> Exo 39:2 He made the ephod of gold, blue, purple, scarlet, and fine twined linen.

Exo 39:3 They beat the gold into thin plates, and cut it into wires, to work it in with the blue, the purple, the scarlet, and the fine linen, the work of the skillful workman.

Exo 39:4 They made shoulder straps for it, joined together. At the two ends it was joined together.

Exo 39:5 The skillfully woven band that was on it, with which to fasten it on, was of the same piece, like its work; of gold, of blue, purple, scarlet, and fine twined linen; as YHWH commanded Moses.

Exo 39:6 They worked the onyx stones, enclosed in settings of gold, engraved with the engravings of a signet, according to the names of the children of Israel.

Exo 39:7 **He put them on the shoulder straps of the ephod, to be stones of memorial for the children of Israel, as YHWH commanded Moses.**

Exo 39:8 He made the breastplate, the work of a skillful workman, like the work of the ephod; of gold, of blue, purple, scarlet, and fine twined linen.

Exo 39:9 It was square. They made the breastplate double. Its length was a span, and its width a span, being double.

Exo 39:10 They set in it four rows of stones. A row of ruby, topaz, and beryl was the first row;

Exo 39:11 and the second row, a turquoise, a sapphire, and an emerald;

Exo 39:12 and the third row, a jacinth, an agate, and an amethyst;

Exo 39:13 and the fourth row, a chrysolite, an onyx, and a jasper. They were enclosed in gold settings.

Exo 39:14 The stones were according to the names of the children of Israel, twelve, according to their names; like the engravings of a signet, everyone according to his name, for the twelve tribes.

Exo 39:15 They made on the breastplate chains like cords, of braided work of pure gold.

Exo 39:16 They made two settings of gold, and two gold rings, and put the two rings on the two ends of the breastplate.

Exo 39:17 They put the two braided chains of gold in the two rings at the ends of the breastplate.

Exo 39:18 The other two ends of the two braided chains they put on the two settings, and put them on the shoulder straps of the ephod, in its front.

Exo 39:19 They made two rings of gold, and put them on the two ends of the breastplate, on its edge, which was toward the side of the ephod inward.

Exo 39:20 They made two more rings of gold, and put them on the two shoulder straps of the ephod underneath, in its front, close by its coupling, above the skillfully woven band of the ephod.

Exo 39:21 They bound the breastplate by its rings to the rings of the ephod with a lace of blue, that it might be on the skillfully woven band of the ephod, and that the breastplate might not come loose from the ephod, as YHWH commanded Moses.

TUESDAY Exo 39:22 He made the robe of the ephod of woven work, all of blue.

Exo 39:23 The opening of the robe in the middle of it was like the opening of a coat of mail, with a binding around its opening, that it should not be torn.

Exo 39:24 They made on the skirts of the robe pomegranates of blue, purple, scarlet, and twined linen.

Exo 39:25 They made bells of pure gold, and put the bells between the pomegranates around the skirts of the robe, between the pomegranates;

Exo 39:26 a bell and a pomegranate, a bell and a pomegranate, around the skirts of the robe, to minister in, as YHWH commanded Moses.

Exo 39:27 They made the coats of fine linen of woven work for Aaron, and for his sons,

Exo 39:28 and the turban of fine linen, and the linen headbands of fine linen, and the linen breeches of fine twined linen,

Exo 39:29 and the sash of fine twined linen, and blue, and purple, and scarlet, the work of the embroiderer, as YHWH commanded Moses.

Exo 39:30 They made the plate of the holy crown of pure gold, and wrote on it a writing, like the engravings of a signet: "HOLY TO YHWH".

Exo 39:31 **They tied to it a lace of blue, to fasten it on the turban above, as YHWH commanded Moses.**

Exo 39:32 Thus all the work of the tabernacle of the Tent of Meeting was finished. The children of Israel did according to all that YHWH commanded Moses; so they did.

WEDNESDAY Exo 39:33 They brought the tabernacle to Moses, the tent, with all its furniture, its clasps, its boards, its bars, its pillars, its sockets,

Exo 39:34 the covering of rams' skins dyed red, the covering of sea cow hides, the veil of the screen,

Exo 39:35 the ark of the testimony with its poles, the mercy seat,

Exo 39:36 the table, all its vessels, the show bread,

Exo 39:37 the pure lamp stand, its lamps, even the lamps to be set in order, all its vessels, the oil for the light,

Exo 39:38 the golden altar, the anointing oil, the sweet incense, the screen for the door of the Tent,

Exo 39:39 the bronze altar, its grating of brass, its poles, all of its vessels, the basin and its base,

Exo 39:40 the hangings of the court, its pillars, its sockets, the screen for the gate of the court, its cords, its pins, all the instruments of the service of the tabernacle, for the Tent of Meeting,

Exo 39:41 the finely worked garments for ministering in the holy place, the holy garments for Aaron the priest, and the garments of his sons, to minister in the priest's office.

Exo 39:42 According to all that YHWH commanded Moses, so the children of Israel did all the work.

Exo 39:43 **Moses saw all the work, and behold, they had done it as YHWH had commanded, even so had they done it: and Moses blessed them.**

The Tabernacle Erected

THURSDAY Exo 40:1 YHWH spoke to Moses, saying,

Exo 40:2 **"On the first day of the first month you shall raise up the tabernacle of the Tent of Meeting.**

Exo 40:3 You shall put the ark of the testimony in it, and you shall screen the ark with the veil.

Exo 40:4 You shall bring in the table, and set in order the things that are on it. You shall bring in the lamp stand, and light its lamps.

Exo 40:5 You shall set the golden altar for incense before the ark of the testimony, and put the screen of the door to the tabernacle.

Exo 40:6 "You shall set the altar of burnt offering before the door of the tabernacle of the Tent of Meeting.

Exo 40:7 You shall set the basin between the Tent of Meeting and the altar, and shall put water therein.

Exo 40:8 You shall set up the court around it, and hang up the screen of the gate of the court.

Exo 40:9 "You shall take the anointing oil, and anoint the tabernacle, and all that is in it, and shall make it holy, and all its furniture: and it will be holy.

Exo 40:10 You shall anoint the altar of burnt offering, with all its vessels, and sanctify the altar: and the altar will be most holy.

Exo 40:11 You shall anoint the basin and its base, and sanctify it.

Exo 40:12 "You shall bring Aaron and his sons to the door of the Tent of Meeting, and shall wash them with water.

Exo 40:13 You shall put on Aaron the holy garments; and you shall anoint him, and sanctify him, that he may minister to me in the priest's office.

Exo 40:14 You shall bring his sons, and put coats on them.

Exo 40:15 You shall anoint them, as you anointed their father, that they may minister to me in the priest's office. Their anointing shall be to them for an everlasting priesthood throughout their generations."

Exo 40:16 Moses did so. According to all that YHWH commanded him, so he did.

Exo 40:17 In the first month in the second year, on the first day of the month, the tabernacle was raised up.

Exo 40:18 Moses raised up the tabernacle, and laid its sockets, and set up its boards, and put in its bars, and raised up its pillars.

Exo 40:19 He spread the covering over the tent, and put the roof of the tabernacle above on it, as YHWH commanded Moses.

Exo 40:20 He took and put the testimony into the ark, and set the poles on the ark, and put the mercy seat above on the ark.

Exo 40:21 He brought the ark into the tabernacle, and set up the veil of the screen, and screened the ark of the testimony, as YHWH commanded Moses.

Exo 40:22 He put the table in the Tent of Meeting, on the side of the tabernacle northward, outside of the veil.

Exo 40:23 He set the bread in order on it before YHWH, as YHWH commanded Moses.

Exo 40:24 He put the lamp stand in the Tent of Meeting, opposite the table, on the side of the tabernacle southward.

Exo 40:25 He lit the lamps before YHWH, as YHWH commanded Moses.

Exo 40:26 He put the golden altar in the Tent of Meeting before the veil;

Exo 40:27 and he burned incense of sweet spices on it, as YHWH commanded Moses.

Exo 40:28 He put up the screen of the door to the tabernacle.

Exo 40:29 He set the altar of burnt offering at the door of the tabernacle of the Tent of Meeting, and offered on it the burnt offering and the meal offering, as YHWH commanded Moses.

Exo 40:30 He set the basin between the Tent of Meeting and the altar, and put water therein, with which to wash.

MY NOTES

Exo 40:31 Moses, Aaron, and his sons washed their hands and their feet there.

Exo 40:32 When they went into the Tent of Meeting, and when they came near to the altar, they washed, as YHWH commanded Moses.

Exo 40:33 He raised up the court around the tabernacle and the altar, and set up the screen of the gate of the court. So Moses finished the work.

The Glory of the Lord

Exo 40:34 Then the cloud covered the Tent of Meeting, and YHWH's glory filled the tabernacle.

Exo 40:35 Moses wasn't able to enter into the Tent of Meeting, because the cloud stayed on it, and YHWH's glory filled the tabernacle.

Exo 40:36 When the cloud was taken up from over the tabernacle, the children of Israel went onward, throughout all their journeys;

Exo 40:37 but if the cloud wasn't taken up, then they didn't travel until the day that it was taken up.

Exo 40:38 For the cloud of YHWH was on the tabernacle by day, and there was fire in the cloud by night, in the sight of all the house of Israel, throughout all their journeys.

VERSE BOXES — EXODUS 40:38

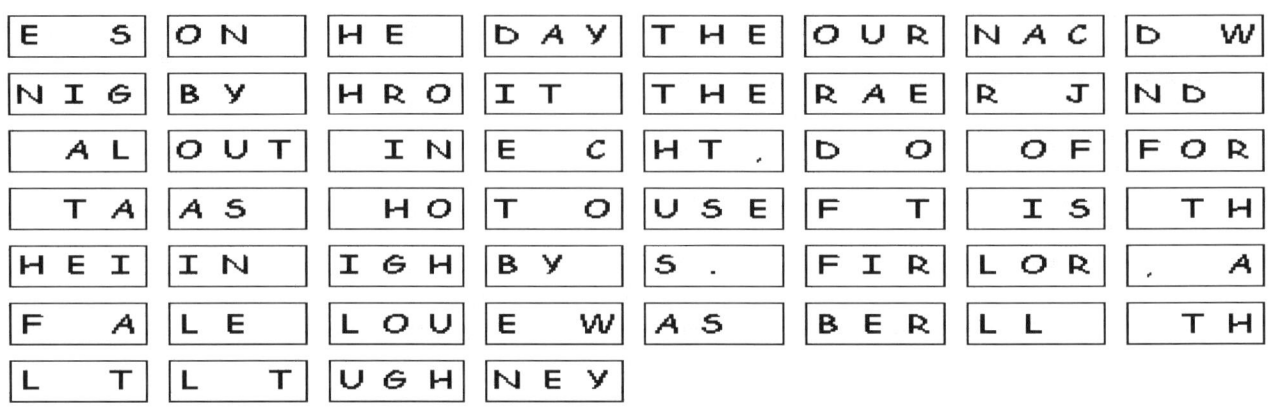

VERSE FIND — EXODUS 40:16

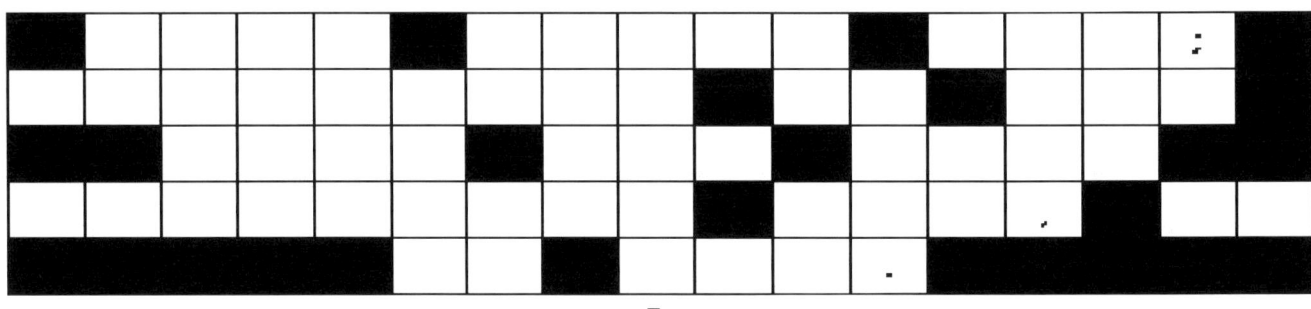

Once again, we pray that this booklet will be a blessing to you and your children and that your children will be a blessing to others.

If you have been blessed by this ministry, please consider donating to TORAH TOWN.

Please continue to keep us in your prayers as we continue to pray for you.

FACEBOOK: https://facebook.com/TorahTown

YOUTUBE: https://youtube.com/TorahTown

WEBSITE: http://torahtown.host22.com

DONATIONS

https://paypal.me/TorahTown

Made in the USA
Coppell, TX
24 December 2020